IMAGES OF WAR

GERMAN GUNS of THE THIRD REICH
1939-1945

RARE PHOTOGRAPHS FROM WARTIME ARCHIVES

IAN BAXTER

Pen & Sword
MILITARY

First published in Great Britain in 2007 by
PEN & SWORD MILITARY
an imprint of
Pen & Sword Books Ltd,
47 Church Street, Barnsley,
South Yorkshire.
S70 2AS

Copyright © Ian Baxter, 2007

ISBN 978-1-84415-567-5

The right of Ian Baxter to be identified as Author of this Work
has been asserted by him in accordance with the
Copyright, Designs and Patents Act 1988.

A CIP catalogue record for this book is available
from the British Library

All rights reserved. No part of this book may be reproduced or transmitted
in any form or by any means, electronic or mechanical including photocopying,
recording or by any information storage and retrieval system,
without permission from the Publisher in writing.

Printed and bound in Great Britain by CPI UK

Pen & Sword Books Ltd incorporates the imprints of
Pen & Sword Aviation, Pen & Sword Maritime,
Pen & Sword Military, Pen & Sword Select, Pen & Sword Military Classics,
Leo Cooper, Wharncliffe Local History

For a complete list of Pen & Sword titles please contact:
PEN & SWORD BOOKS LIMITED
47 Church Street, Barnsley, South Yorkshire, S70 2AS, England.
E-mail: enquiries@pen-and-sword.co.uk
Website: www.pen-and-sword.co.uk

Contents

Photographic Acknowledgements

It is with the greatest pleasure that I use this opportunity on concluding this book to thank those who helped make this volume possible. My expression of gratitude first goes to my German photographic collector Rolf Halfen. He has been an unfailing source; supplying me with a number of very rare artillery photographs that were obtained from numerous private sources. Throughout the research stage of this book Rolf searched and contacted numerous collectors all over Germany, trying in vain to find a multitude of interesting and rare photographs.

Further afield in Poland I am also extremely grateful to Marcin Kaludow, my Polish photographic specialist, who supplied me with a great number of rare photographs that he sought from private photographic collections in Poland, Russia and the Ukraine. The images he found show a host of interesting photographs like the 60cm Mörser `Thor`, which was one of the largest pieces of field equipment to see service in the Second World War.

Finally, I wish to display my kindness and appreciation to my American photographic collector, Richard White, who supplied me with a number of rare unpublished photographs especially showing the various 8.8cm Flak guns that were deployed on the Eastern and Western Fronts both in an anti-tank and anti-aircraft role.

All other images in this book are credited to the HITM Archive
www.htm-archive.co.uk

A halftrack towing an 8.8cm flak gun with a full compliment of crew travels across a field ready to re-position itself for further action.

Introduction

Historically, the use of artillery refers to any engine used for the discharge of projectiles under combat conditions. The term also describes ground-based troops with the primary function of manning such weapons. The word artillery is derived from the old French verb *attilier*, meaning '*to equip*'. This term includes coastal artillery, which traditionally defended coastal areas against seaborne attack and controlled the passage of ships using their ability to deny access through the threat of coastal fire. It also includes land-based field artillery. When powered flight was introduced during the First World War, artillery also included ground-based anti-aircraft fired from anti-aircraft batteries as well.

The first type of weapon to be used in warfare that was similar to that of the artillery pieces seen on the battlefields of Europe in the Twentieth century was the Bombards. This was the earliest of gunpowder artillery and was distinguished by its lack of a field carriage. After the development of the Bombard came the cannon, which was a lethal cast iron weapon which was designed with a dedicated field carriage with axle, trail and horse-drawn limber. This produced mobile field pieces that could move and support an army in action rather than being found only in siege and static defences. The cannon were always muzzle-loaders, casting technology having standardised and removed the often-dangerous breach-loading design. Its operation was still a complex technical task, often undertaken at high-speed and in stressful conditions, where a mistake could easily be lethal. The field carriage eased movement in general, but traverse and elevation were still very limited and slow.

From the 1860s artillery was soon forced into a series of rapid technological and operational changes that saw the development of modern artillery. Modern artillery itself was distinguished by its large calibre, which fired an explosive shell or rocket projectile, and was of such a size and weight that it required a specialised mount for firing and transport. Cannon artillery such as the howitzer, mortar, and the field gun were deemed modern artillery. The types of cannon artillery are generally distinguished by the velocity at which they fired projectiles. Naval guns or infantry support guns are typically longer-barrelled, low-trajectory, high-velocity weapons designed primarily for a direct-fire role. Typically the length of a cannon barrel is greater than 25 times its calibre (inner diameter). Howitzers, however, are relatively shorter, capable of both high- and low-angle fire. A howitzer was capable of firing a high-trajectory projectile, allowing it to hit a target behind hills and ridges, as well as penetrating concrete bunker emplacements. These weapons are most often employed in an indirect-fire role, capable of operating in defilade. Typically, the length of a howitzer cannon is between 15 and 25 times its calibre. Mortars are smaller, low-velocity, high-angle weapons capable of only high-trajectory fire at a relatively short range. Typically the length of a mortar barrel is less than 15 times its calibre.

Modern field artillery can be divided into two other categories; towed and self-propelled. Towed artillery has a prime mover, usually a tractor or armoured tracked vehicle, to move the piece, crew, and ammunition from one part of the front to another. Self-propelled howitzers are permanently mounted on a carriage or vehicle with room for the crew and ammunition. These weapons are more than capable of moving independently in order to move quickly from one firing position to another in order to support the mobile attack and to avoid counter-battery fire. There are also mortar carrier vehicles, many of which allow the mortar to be removed from the vehicle and be used dismounted, potentially in terrain in which the vehicle cannot navigate or in order to avoid detection.

Out on the battlefield all these weapons could be used in a variety of roles, depending obviously on the calibre of the weapons. Field artillery for instance was used to support armies in the field. Howitzers, on the other hand were generally used in direct support of infantry and armor, where the guns of a battery or even a battalion were employed to fire simultaneously onto a single point or area target. Anti-aircraft weapons were another important piece of artillery and were used generally to protect the ground troops from aerial attack. These flak weapons were usually mobile and not fixed, and were primarily designed for attacking aircraft from the ground. Some guns were suitable for dual-role anti-aircraft and field (anti-tank) use. The German 8.8cm flak gun is one very famous weapon that was used extensively throughout the Second World War in a dual aerial and ground role. But it was one of many various German guns that were designed and manufactured to see action on the front lines.

The origins of the development of German infantry guns begun during World War One. At the beginning of the war, the field artillery of the German Army had only two main types of guns: the light 7.7cm Field Cannon 96 n. A, and the 10.5cm Field Howitzer 98/09. The use of both these guns on the battlefield was relatively effective, but gun crews soon recognized they needed specific guns designed with good overall performances in order to over come strong opposition. In some circumstances they found that when waging an attack, individual guns had proven so ineffective that enemy positions were still intact after the artillery shells had been fired.

The invention of using artillery on the battlefield had been a very important step in modern warfare and was used primarily to clear the way for the main attack for the infantry, and later the armoured vehicles. The Germans believed that artillery fire must not check the momentum of the attack. The mission of the artillery preparation before the main attack was to destroy, or at least to

At the moment of firing the gunnery officer is seen raising his arm signalling to fire as the 15cm howitzers projectile leaves the barrel during action on the Eastern Front in the summer of 1941.

An SS battery of 15cm IG33 howitzers more than likely in action during operations in France in 1940. The gun was widely used by both the Wehrmacht and Waffen-SS, especially during the earlier part of the war, but it was still seen in service until 1945.

neutralise, the opponent's defensive positions in the area between the line of contact and the regimental reserve line. However, the Germans found that their guns and tactics employed on the battlefield were unable to affect the situation decisively, and as a consequence the enemy were able to hinder the following infantry attack.

In spite of the numerous problems incurred by the Germans and the use of their artillery, they were determined to go on and develop a range of powerful guns in spite of the Versailles Treaty thoroughly disrupting the German armament industry. The two principal manufactures, Friedrich Krupp AG and Rheinische Metallwaaren und Maschinenfabrik (later Rheinische Borsig AG) were limited in designs they could produce. However, once the Nazi party came to power in January 1933 the restrictions on armament production were almost abandoned overnight. Initially the development on various guns were put into production and tested, but these guns were soon redeveloped and existing designs reworked. By the late 1930's artillery equipment of the Wehrmacht was standardised on a few calibres, and the weapons designed and manufactured were well-tested and suitable for combat conditions. The army's field weapons were of 10.5cm, 15cm and 21cm calibres. Anti-aircraft or flak weapons were 3.7cm light guns, 8.8cm medium gun and 10.5cm heavy guns. Anti-tank or Pak weapons were the 3.7cm gun and a 7.92mm anti-tank rifle for infantry use. Tried and tested, these German guns would now be used in anger against their enemies in Europe.

Chapter One

Structure and Training

Before the outbreak of war in September 1939 the establishment of the divisional artillery consisted of one field regiment of three batteries, one medium regiment of three batteries and one medium of two batteries, one of which were either mechanised or horse-drawn. The field regiment contained a regimental headquarters, a signals section, three field batteries and one medium battery. The field batteries had a battery headquarters, a survey section, a signals section, and three troops with an ammunition column. The troops had a troop headquarters, a signals section, transport and ammunition sections, and two gun sections with two 10.5cm howitzers. Quite frequently a section had two 2cm anti-aircraft guns attached for local air defence. The medium battery consisted of a battery headquarters, a signals section, a survey section, and troops with two 15cm howitzers and one 10cm gun. In many cases two 2cm anti-aircraft guns were attached. The total strength of the divisional artillery was 89 officers, 2,516 men and 1,785 horses including a number of motorised vehicles. It consisted of some 48 guns

During a ceremony at a training barracks in early 1939. A commanding officer can be seen standing on a podium flanked by two 10.5cm guns. These guns were the standard divisional artillery piece, in its original form.

At a barracks a commanding officer appears to be issuing orders of the day to a group of artillerymen prior to manoeuvres in early 1939. A 10.5cm le FH 18 gun can be seen with a caisson attached to a limber. Note the letter `D` for `Dora` painted in white on the splinter shield.

and howitzers and 24 small-calibre anti-aircraft guns. The motorised infantry division contained relatively the same allocation but the units were all mechanised.

An armoured division consisted of one regiment of two fully mechanised batteries, a total of 47 officers, 1065 men and 24 guns. However, this establishment later incorporated a third battery of 15cm howitzers. In a mountain division the regiment contained a headquarters, a signals section, and two batteries each of three troops. The troops had at least four 7.5cm mountain guns each. As for moving the guns from one part of the front to another, the mountain troops or Gebirgsjäger was chiefly comprised of pack mules that transported the weapons across some of the most inhospitable terrain.

In Germany and Austria those regiments that made up the divisional artillery had been put through vigorous training in the various artillery training regiment barracks and artillery depot regiments. A typical artillery recruit would have learnt the significance of military rank structures and basic drill movements. He would be extremely fit and he would also be accustomed to wearing uniform. Good basic training equipped the recruit for combat service and, in addition to familiar exercises such as drill movements and firearms training, exercises under live fire were widely used. Even for artillerymen, basic infantry training was essential. If a gun had been knocked out of action or run out of ammunition, the artilleryman would have to fend for himself.

On completion of his basic training, the recruit commenced specialist artillery training. First the individual would receive his own training and would learn about the variety of artillery weapons in service, both of native design and of captured models. This was followed by learning all about the specifications of the type of gun and cartridge cases he would be using. With all this knowledge the recruits would come together and exercise as a team. Trained crews would take part in unit level exercises and then finally the units themselves would be involved in large-scale manoeuvres. In addition to basic artillery training, specialisation courses were run for

During training exercise a group of artillerymen practice with the use of horse drawn transport towing a caisson attached to a limber and artillery piece. Although the *Wehrmacht* intended making this army an all mechanised armoured force, through the war they still depended on the horse for over eighty-percent of motive power.

Artillerymen men are training with horse drawn artillery pieces. Even by 1939 the Wehrmacht's main mode of towing artillery was by horse. Preparing artillery for action on the battlefield would rely heavily on the horse, especially between 1939 and 1942.

A training exercise during the early winter of 1939. Here artillerymen can be seen with caisson attached to artillery. In the artillery regiments a riding horse was referred to as a 'Warmblüter' (warm-blooded), quick agile, light horse.

An artillery battery on exercise in the early summer of 1939. Artillery training was gruelling but, during the war, artillery firepower became a key player in defensive and offensive success of both the Wehrmacht and Waffen-SS.

those recruits looking to become officer candidates. There were extensive courses for those wanting to train and ride with horses. There were even courses for those eager to learn about instrument readings with an azimuth. Courses on meteorology were also taught to recruits that wanted to learn about the necessary data concerning temperature, wind, and barometric pressure. The majority of the recruits, however, did not undertake any specialised training. Instead, they were taught how to load and transport the ammunition, the art of priming the shells, and finally firing them.

The most important part of artillery training, apart from the technical training on how to operate the gun itself, was on how to use the gun as an efficient fighting weapon. Training manuals were produced and during the war more training literature was written based on combat experience on the Eastern Front. But from the very beginning of the training, even during peacetime, each recruit had been lectured extensively on the operational principles of the German offensive doctrine. The teachers regarded tactics and logistics as the main task of an artilleryman. Their sole objective was to combine arms in attack and to bring its armoured forces and the infantry into decisive action against the enemy with sufficient firepower and shock. Superiority in force and firepower, as well as the surprise element, was to play

Artillery regiment troops pose at their barracks with a 7.5cm FK 16 n.A gun. This weapon dated back to the First World War and was revamped for use against Poland in 1939. It was originally intended as a horse drawn cavalry-accompanying gun, but was eventually found in any type of formation needing a light gun.

a great part in an offensive. Artillery support was regarded as of decisive importance for the preparation and the successful conduct of an attack. The Germans believed that the artillery fire must not check the momentum of the attack. Consequently, the heaviest fire was to fall well ahead of the advancing force. The mission of each artilleryman was the preparation of his artillery before the attack. Counter-battery fire on enemy artillery located in positions which commanded the ground over which the main attack was to be made, was of decisive importance. The artillery regiments were taught that their objective was to pave a path of fire and destruction and to allow the main attacking force through. Whilst the armoured force and infantry moved forward along the path opened by the artillery, the artillery was to use counter-battery fire. As the attack progressed, engaging successive lines of anti-tank defence, the artillery were to screen the flanks of the attack with heavy shelling. Once the attack was in full progress, anti-tank and anti-aircraft guns were the first to move forward, followed by the artillery that were towed either by horse-limbers or half tracked vehicles.

Artillerymen at a training barracks wearing their familiar white training garments can be seen cleaning their 10.5cm le. FH 18 howitzer. All artillery crews were taught to maintain and clean their weapons regularly.

An SS gun crew training with a 7.5cm le IG light infantry artillery piece. This weapon was one of the first post World War One guns to be issued to the Wehrmacht and later the SS. The gun was light and robust and employed a shotgun breech action.

A Wehrmacht 10.5cm gun crew are being sworn in during a passing-out ceremony. These new artillerymen were now ready for action. They had been taught how to load and transport the ammunition, the art of priming shells, and finally how to fire their weapon in anger.

A battery located in the snow are undertaking training with the 7.5cm le IG 18. All of these guns had a fitted splinter shield and had either wood-spoked type wheels or steel discs with pneumatic tyres, depending upon whether the gun was to be horse or vehicle drawn.

A photograph taken the moment a 7.5cm le IG 18 fires a projectile during a training exercise. These guns fired a standard high explosive shell weighing some 6kgs. Because the gun was light it was very mobile and allowed infantry to use it for close support.

A 7.5cm le IG 18 and crew during a training exercise. The weapon has steel discs with pneumatic tyres suggesting that the gun has been towed to its position by a vehicle. The use of pneumatic tyres reduced wear and tear and allowed the gun to be transported quicker.

Leading elements of an artillery regiment have halted inside a German town during manoeuvres in the winter of 1939. A halftrack prime mover can be seen towing a 10.5cm howitzer. A support vehicle more than likely carrying the ammunition is also following the column.

An interesting photograph showing an SS artillery training barracks in 1939. With the draped national and SS flags, a podium and artillery pieces, the photograph suggests this to be a ceremonial occasion for an unidentified SS artillery regiment.

Here SS artillerymen are being lectured during a training exercise. The first SS artillery regiment emerged in 1939 to serve the SS-Verfügungs Division drawn from the SS Verfügungstruppe.

On manoeuvres are artillerymen of the SS.Polizei-Artillery-Regiment. The men are on a march wearing their distinctive white denim training tunics with field grey trousers The long column of artillery limbers and caissons are churning up dust clouds, which during combat conditions could easily be detected from the air by an enemy aircraft.

An SS artillery crew undergoing intensive training with their 15cm s IG 33 gun. This particular infantry gun was a reliable and robust weapon, but was relatively heavy especially for training purposes.

Wearing their typical pea-pattern smocks these SS artillerymen are cleaning their artillery piece. During training commanders had instilled in their recruits that all guns were to be kept in pristine condition, both for prestige purposes of the battery, and to avoid mechanical problems with the gun. A clean gun was essential for a shell to be fired safely and accurately.

An SS artilleryman is cleaning one of the components of a 7.5cm le IG 18. When the Waffen-SS formally came into existence in March 1940 the three divisions – the SS-Verfügungs, Totenkopf and SS.Polizei – each possessed an artillery regiment equipped with 36 light field guns, but lacked any heavy artillery.

An SS artillery crew are maintaining their 7.5cm le IG 18 by thoroughly cleaning the external and internal workings of the weapon. The guns required constant cleaning and maintenance. The general cleaning methods were primitive, labour intensive and time-consuming, and were prone to human negligence especially when out on the battlefield. Dismounting the gun barrel to thoroughly clean it from copper residues also consumed a lot of time and manpower.

An SS.Polizei crew belonging to a 10.5cm howitzer battery located in a muddy field prepare to open fire on a rainy day. This photograph was taken on exercise and shows the crew preparing to load the gun with a shell. Note the gun layer checking the gun sight or azimuth for distance and accuracy.

On the practice range with the elevation set the gun layer checks the sight before ordering the crew to load and fire the 10.5cm howitzer. The battery officer who was responsible for the proper carrying-out of firing commands and fire orders can be seen standing on the left. The crewman on the right is more than likely the gunner.

An official armament inspection is being made to an artillery barracks in 1939. A number of Nazi officials can be seen watching a 10.5cm howitzer crew undertake a gun loading procedure.

Gun crews all wearing the familiar waterproof Zeltbahn are being given instruction on the technical capability of the 3.7cm Pak 36. This gun was the standard German anti-tank gun at the outbreak of the Second World War. It was introduced in 1936 and small numbers were first sent to Spain for field trials during the Spanish Civil War.

A 15cm heavy field gun has been manhandled out of a shed on its carriage in the snow. This gun remained the principle heavy field howitzer throughout World War Two. It was of conventional design with a split-trail carriage.

The crew of a 7.5cm FK 16nA pose for the camera during an exercise in 1939. The battery officer can be seen standing next to the gun's spoked wheel. In action this old First World War gun weighed some 15-tons and had a maximum range of 12,875m.

Chapter Two

Infantry Guns

The Germans introduced a number of artillery pieces for the infantry prior to and during the Second World War. The principle lines of development in these guns were intended to provide a reliable and proven weapon with a good range that was conventional in concept and also simple and robust. The German infantry artillery formed the main organic support of the division and supported the combat troops prior to and during action. It was of paramount importance that these infantry field guns used on the battlefield were light and manoeuvrable. The main lighter infantry field guns used at the outbreak of war were the 7.5cm and 10.5cm calibre guns.

The 7.5cm leichtes Infanteriegeschütz 18 or 7.5cm le IG 18 was one of the first 7.5cm calibre artillery weapons to be issued to the German Army after the First World War. It was developed by Rheinmetall and was seen on the firing ranges in 1927. The field gun was light and mobile and employed a shotgun breech action. The barrel was installed in a square section casing within another that carried the fixed breechblock and firing mechanism. The gun carriage was simply constructed with a box trail with a spade. A steel splinter shield was fitted and the two wheels attached were either of wood-spoked type or steel discs with pneumatic tyres. A hydro pneumatic recoil system was attached in the cradle below the barrel.

In 1937 a light and more versatile version of this gun was introduced and was known as the 7.5cm le Gebirg IG 18 (Obermühl). It was specifically developed for the mountain troops or Gebirgsjäger, and was almost identical to the earlier model, but the carriage had a light tubular trail, no shield, and lightweight spoked wheels. It was designed to be quickly dismantled into six mule-pack or ten-pack loads, where the Gebirgsjäger troops could then easily transport it across various terrain including mountains.

After the fall of France in June 1940 the 7.5cm IG 38 had become outdated and the German Army requested a gun with greater range and better anti-tank capability. In response to these calls Krupp designed the 7.5cm IG 42. The gun had a tubular split trail, pneumatic tyres, a splinter shield and a cage-type muzzle brake. Although the IG 42 gun was not built on a large scale the crews that used it found it had a reasonable performance and was seen in action on the Eastern Front. In

1944 a later version of this gun was designed.

Another 7.5cm gun to see action was the mountain guns or Gebirgskanone. The first production type that went into service and was used by the Gebirgsjäger was the 7.5cm Gebirgskanone 15 or 7.5cm Geb K 15. These Skoda produced guns were mainly used during the occupation of Yugoslavia. The entire weapon broke into seven pack loads, the heaviest weighing some 156kg.

One of the most popular 7.5cm mountain guns that remained in service throughout the war was the 7.5cm Gebirgsgeschütz 36. Rheinmetall-Borsig AG designed this well-liked gun, and it entered service in 1938. The gun had a split trail and the recoil system was a variable system that automatically shortened the recoil as the elevation increased. The disc wheels were lightweight with solid rubber tyres, though some had wood-spoked wheels. There was no splinter shield due to the fact that the gun was primarily designed for mountain use. With no shield this helped to keep the weight low and enabled the whole weapon to be broken down into eight loads relatively quickly.

In the German Army various other 7.5cm guns had been employed on the battlefield. One weapon in particular to enter service had dated back to World War I and was renamed and redesigned as the 7.5cm Feldkanone 16 neuer Art or 7.5cm FK 16nA. It was originally intended as a horse-drawn cavalry-accompanying gun, but it eventually found itself with any type of formation needing a light gun. This particular 7.5cm weapon never saw extensive action and was hardly seen in Russia by 1943. Even the gun's replacement, the 7.5cm leichte Feldkanone 18 or 7.5cm le FK 18 failed to improve so far as range and velocity were concerned. Nevertheless, it still remained in service throughout the war.

An improvement on the 7.5cm FK 18 was the 7.5cm Feldkanone 38 or 7.5cm FK 38. This particular gun was based on the same general design as the FK 18, but the barrel was longer and it had a cylindrical muzzle brake with five rows of six slots.

Although the 7.5cm infantry gun was widely used during the war it remained in limited production, despite it being cheap and easy to produce. The next calibre gun to see extensive action during the war, especially until 1943, was the army's original standard field howitzer, the 10.5cm leichte Feldhaubitze. The first 10.5cm gun to be used throughout the war successfully was the 10.5cm leichte Feldhaubitze 18 or 10.5cm le FH 18 (Opladen). The gun had a good reputation as a reliable and stable weapon that was easy to manoeuvre and use. The carriage had a split trail pattern with folding spades, and had either pressed metal or wood-spoked wheels. But in spite of the satisfactory performance it still fell short in the matter of maximum range, especially against the British 25-pounder field gun and later the Russian 7.62mm M1939 divisional gun.

In 1942 a new version of the 10.5cm FH 18 was introduced known as the 10.5cm

Here a battery of Gebirgsjäger artillery has elevated their 7.5cm Geb G36 mountain guns ready for action. Within the ranks of the Gebirgsjäger these weapons were robust and well liked.

leichte Feldhaubitze 18/40 or 10.5cm le FH18/40 (Drachenfels). This was followed by 10.5cm le FH 18/42, 10.5cm le FH 42, and the 10.5cm le FH 43. The various improvements on these 10.5cm guns were for the most part rather uninspired. As for all the field and medium infantry artillery employed on the battlefield they had been developed specifically for increasing the barrel length which, together with better propellant, gave greater muzzle velocity and accuracy. Many of these guns had been redesigned under the stress of wartime and as a result suffered with various degrees of delays and constant hardware problems. In fact, by 1944 there were never enough guns to ago around and even captured stocks rarely made up the shortfall.

A group of Gebirgsjäger troops are manhandling a 7.5cm Geb G36 mountain gun through the snow during winter operations on the Eastern Front in 1941. It appears that the gun has skis attached to the platform in order to help the crew move it across the arctic terrain.

Gebirgs troops appear to have utilised a captured Soviet gun and are moving it through the snow. This particular artillery piece was not widely used by the mountain troops as it was too heavy and bulky and required excessive manpower to move it across the snow.

The crew of a 7.5cm Geb 36 mountain gun make last minute preparations before moving their weapon into place and firing. Note the gun barrel has a perforated muzzlebrake. This gun type remained in service throughout the war.

A photograph taken the moment the crew fire a 7.5cm Geb G36 mountain gun. The authorised gun strength of a Gebirgs division consisted of some 4 heavy infantry guns, 39 anti-tank guns, 12 light field or mountain howitzers and 12 heavy field howitzers.

Here a 10.5cm gun crew are preparing to open fire on a target during operations in Russia in the autumn of 1941. One of the gunners is about to look through the gun sight in order to give the crew accurate information relating to the correct range and elevation needed to fire the gun.

A crew stands by for a fire mission with their 10.5cm howitzer. Like so many artillerymen a great deal of time was spent waiting. During these endless periods of time the crews were kept busy by displacing to firing positions, cleaning the gun tube and other parts of the weapon, and tending to the horses.

During operations in Poland in September 1939. Here a 10.5cm gun crew pose for the camera with two skinned dead animals that will more than likely be prepared for their evening meal. Note that a tarpaulin has been draped on the right wheel of the gun. This was done in order to afford some camouflage protection by breaking up the shape of the gun.

An interesting photograph showing various modes of artillery transportation used during the Polish campaign in 1939. The vehicles have been carrying the 7.5cm FK 16 n.A gun. One of the artillery pieces can be seen stowed on board the vehicle on the left, whilst the vehicles on the right are in the process of unloading the guns. Note the ramp used to unload one of the weapons.

A 10.5cm gun being attached to a horse drawn limber during early operations on the Eastern Front in 1941. Even by this period of the war a great number of horses were still utilised for towing artillery to the forward edge of the battlefield.

A 10.5cm howitzer is being readied for action during the campaign in France in May 1940. Foliage has been attached to the spoked wheels, splinter shield, barrel and trail spades.

A horse drawn 10.5cm howitzer with caisson crosses a stone built bridge during operations in France in 1940. Crewmen can clearly be seen riding on the caisson. However, sometimes the crew had to follow on foot to reduce the weight, especially over rough ground.

One of the most popular forms of camouflaging weapons and vehicles was the extensive use of foliage, as seen here on this 10.5cm gun. This not only broke up the distinctive shape, but also helped it blend with in with the local terrain.

Some artillery crews went to great lengths to conceal their weapons from both ground and aerial observation. Here in this photograph one can just make-out the shape of a 10.5cm howitzer in its elevated position.

The 10.5cm howitzer has just recoiled after firing at a target, and the smoke residue can be seen slowly moving across the battery. Note the leather straps used on the artillery crewman helmets. This was to allow the helmet to be camouflaged with foliage.

The crew of a 10.5cm howitzer pose for the camera during a lull in the fighting in May 1940. It was primarily the artillery regiments that were given the task of destroying enemy positions and fortified defences and of conducting counter-battery fire prior to an armoured or infantry assault.

One of the crewmen is poised to load a projectile in the 10.5cm gun during the campaign against France in the summer of 1940. Although these howitzers provided armour piecing and shaped-charge anti-tank rounds, these guns were far from being effective anti-tank weapons.

During a training exercise in 1940 a 10.5cm gun is fired, but the gun barrel has not yet recoiled. The weapon is under the supervision of an umpire who is wearing a white armband. Note the commander or Wachtmeister who is holding a report or map in his hand.

This photo depicts a 10.5cm gun being fired with the barrel already in full recoil. Though the 10.5cm howitzer was a highly regarded artillery piece its maximum range was still limited especially against the British 25-pounder and later the standard Soviet 76.2mm M1939 field gun.

A 10.5cm howitzer is being prepared for action. Combat experience soon showed that artillery support was of decisive importance in the preparation and successful conduct of an attack.

During a training exercise and the photograph captures the moment a 10.5cm howitzer is fired. The umpire wearing his white armband supervises the firing and makes sure the gun crew are undertaking their firing procedures, as taught in the classroom.

A 10.5cm gun is fired and the battery officer can be seen watching the procedure. Although the gun is out in the open artillerymen were trained to conceal their weapons, only moving into firing positions at the last moment.

A posed photograph of a battery commander with his 7.5cm FK 16 n.A. The battery commander oversaw and ensured that artillery crews were strictly and properly carrying out their tasks, whilst at the same time making sure they maintained discipline whilst in action.

The crew of a 10.5cm le. FH16 have well concealed their light field howitzer prior to going into action. The projectiles and their packing tubes are beside the gun. These artillerymen are attached to an SS.Polizei Artillery Regiment during the winter of 1942 in Russia.

During the winter of 1942 and the crew of a 10.5cm le. FH16 pose for the camera with their gun. The howitzer was a relatively short-barrelled piece of weaponry capable of firing a high-trajectory projectile, allowing it to hit targets behind hills and ridges as well as strong defensive positions like concrete bunker systems.

The crew of a 10.5cm le. FH16 pose for the camera with one of the crewman holding a projectile. Two of the crewman can be seen using the specially fitted seats welded to the front of the gun's splinter shield.

A 10.5cm le. FH16 howitzer is well concealed at the entrance of a long framed shelter during operations in Russia on the Northern Front in 1942. The 10.5cm howitzer was a general artillery piece used to attack various targets. Its main targets were the enemy's frontline positions or attacking forces.

The crew from an SS-Polizei artillery regiment have hastily set-up positions with their field howitzer inside a dilapidated barn during operations on the Eastern Front in 1942.

An artillery crew of a 10.5cm howitzer pose for the camera during winter operations on the Leningrad Front in 1942. These men, more than likely from an SS.Polizei artillery regiment, are wearing the new Waffen-SS winter clothing.

A 10.5cm howitzer with its barrel in its elevated position has been well concealed in the snow. Branches too have been attached to the weapon in order to increase its concealment, and the crew have constructed a bunker in the snow next to the gun.

Artillerymen have their photo taken with their well-camouflaged 10.5cm howitzer on the Leningrad Front in 1942. Some of the men are wearing Wehrmacht winter clothing that consisted of a hooded jacket, trousers and mittens.

A 10.5cm howitzer crew prepare to fire their gun on the Eastern Front in the summer of 1942. Note the red-and white-striped aiming stake attached to the gun trail. The aiming stakes were set up some distance forward from the gun to serve as a reference point from which to set the gun's deflection.

The gun crew of a 10.5cm le. FH18 during the French campaign in May 1940. This gun was a robust and reliable weapon. The carriage was of the split trail pattern with folding spades, and either had wood-spoked or pressed metal wheels.

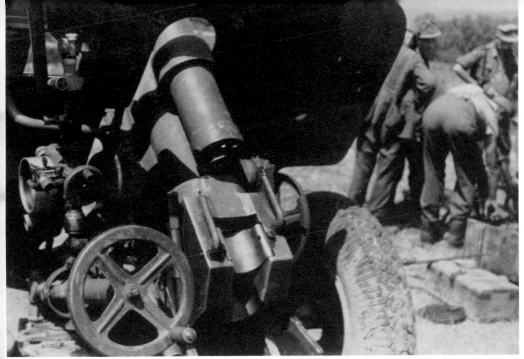

A close-up view of the breech end of a 10.5cm howitzer in 1943. It shows the hand wheel, the gun sight, the gun breech, the splinter shield and one of the tyres.

During the French campaign in 1940 the crew of a 7.5cm le. IG18 conceal their weapon in some undergrowth. Although the gun was one of the first post World War One weapons to be issued to the Wehrmacht, it remained in service until the end of the Second World War in 1945.

A telescopic aiming device tripod has been erected in the snow. The telescopic aiming device was set-up forward of the artillery position by the aimers. Once in position the aimer would attach the telescope to the tripod. This allowed the aimers to set angles in a horizontal plane and panoramic sighting in 360 degrees.

The crew of a 7.5cm le. IG18 prepare their gun for action during operations in France in May 1940. This weapon could not only be fired quickly and accurately but also had an advantage on the battlefield by having a low profile design and splinter shield.

SS.Polizei artillerymen during a lull in the fighting in January 1942. The following month the units of the Polizei division had the `SS` prefix added to their designations. The division itself was re-designated SS.Polizei-Division. The rifle regiments were also re-designated as SS.Infantry-Regiments 1, 2, and 3.

Artillerymen with their camouflaged 10.5cm howitzer on the Eastern Front in the winter of 1942. The crew is from an unidentified SS.Polizei artillery regiment. The SS.Polizei artillery regiments saw extensive action in the Wolchow River area, which was defended by the Soviet 2nd Assault Army.

A battery of 10.5cm howitzers being prepared for action under simulated battle conditions in March 1940. Note the covered aluminum bucket used by the crew for unused propellant charges. Gunners preferred Aluminum to the use of Steel in order to prevent a spark from igniting the charges.

The rear of a 10.5cm howitzer more than likely being towed by horse drawn transport. Even by 1941 a number of divisions were still allotted with few motorized vehicles and as a consequence the bulk of the artillery were moved to the front by animal draught.

An artillery crew prepares their 10.5cm le. FH18 howitzer for operations in early June 1940. This crew belongs to an SS.Polizei artillery regiment. The SS division participated in the second phase of the French campaign, where they were initially held in reserve.

The moment a shell is loaded into the chamber of a 10.5cm howitzer. Note the rammer with his ramming rod and another artilleryman handling a cartridge case. When the projectile was placed into the chamber, it was followed by the rammer who used the ramming rod to set the projectile into the chamber, and then to be followed by placing a cartridge case full of propellant.

An SS gun crew with their 7.5cm le. IG 18 during the Western campaign in May 1940. The gun weighed 400kg and fired a 6kg shell to a maximum range of 3,375m. It remained the standard light infantry gun throughout the war.

SS troops move their guns into position along a dirt track during operations in France in 1940. Two-7.5cm le. IG 18 guns are brought forward followed by a 10.5cm howitzer. Both Wehrmacht and Waffen-SS generally assigned light field guns or pack howitzers to dedicated infantry fire support, though still remaining under artillery control.

SS light infantry gun crews with their 7.5cm le. IG 18 guns prepare for a firing mission. These small light highly mobile infantry guns were more than capable of providing SS grenadiers with vital offensive and defensive fire support, particularly when heavier artillery was unavailable.

Knocked out of action on the Eastern Front in 1942 is a 10.5cm le. FH18 light field howitzer. The crew has well concealed the gun in heavy undergrowth and surrounding trees, but has not prevented it from being totally destroyed by Red Army counter-battery fire.

Two crewmembers of a 10.5cm le. FH18 light field howitzer pose for the camera during a lull in the fighting on the Eastern Front in 1942. The gun weighed nearly two tons and fired a 14.4kg shell to a maximum range of 10,675m.

A 10.5cm le. FH18 light field howitzer at dawn in early June 1940. More than 5,000 of these light field howitzers entered service when the war broke out in 1939, and remained the standard light divisional howitzer throughout the war.

Waffen-SS gunners move their 7.5cm le. IG18 light infantry gun to prepare it for another action against Red Army troops in the winter of 1941. Offensively, these guns were designed to accompany attacking troops and even provide direct fire if necessary.

Chapter Three

Heavy Guns

The heaviest field guns in the German Army still capable of being moved about by their crews were the 10cm guns and 15cm howitzers. The 10cm Kanone 18 for instance was a very heavy piece of weaponry and for this reason was designed primarily for horse or vehicle traction. The gun was a simple one-piece barrel inside a jacket with a typical horizontal sliding block and a cage-type muzzle brake. The carriage was a split-trail type with pressed steel disc wheels with solid tyres that were connected with spring-leaf suspension fitted with two spring balancing-presses. For transportation the barrel was disconnected from the recoil system and hauled back to the end of the cradle, where it was secured. The gun was then moved by a wire rope and hand-winched to the carriage. For horse transportation the barrel was removed from the cradle on to wheeled transport, the carriage forming a second load.

Apart from using the 10cm K 18 in a field artillery role the weapon was also designed to be deployed as an emergency coast artillery gun, and a special ranging projectile was manufactured for this role.

The partner to the 10cm K 18, using the same carriage, was the 15cm schwere Feldhaubitze 18 or 15cms s FH 18 (Immergrün). The guns were almost identical expect for the barrel dimensions and the fact that it became the first weapon to be issued with a rocket-assisted shell. The shell was issued in 1941 and was used only for a short period in Russia until it was withdrawn from service.

Another variation of the 15cm heavy field gun to see service, which was lighter than the s FH 18, was the 15cm Schwere Feldhaubitze 36 or 15cm s FH36. This gun was very adaptable on the battlefield and could be transported by horses. The barrel of the gun was slightly shorter than that of the s FH 18 and was originally fitted with a cylindrical muzzlebrake. A quick release connection attached the breech-ring to the recoil system piston rods so that the gun could quickly be disconnected and drawn back onto the cradle extension for travelling. The gun's mobility, firing range and effectiveness with a good projectile weight made the s FH 18 the main weapon of the army division. The gun was used in Poland, on the Western Front in 1940 and on the Eastern Front a year later. Its service on the battlefield proved a success, but the crews found the gun too heavy. By 1943 only a few of these guns remained in active service and were used mainly in Russia until the end of the war.

As with most of the infantry guns that were developed before and during the war, further improvements and new designs were introduced in order to produce guns that were cost effective, reliable, accurate and most of all damaging to the enemy. One such gun that was developed, that heralded a completely new trend in German gun design, was the 15cm schwere Feldhaubitze 18/43 or 15cm s FH 18/43. Many designs were introduced on this gun to economise, but at the same time it was developed with accuracy and effectiveness. One of the main features of the gun, which was different from the usual combination of using an old carriage with a new barrel, was the firing of the projectiles from what was known as a bag-charge loading system. This enabled the crews to fire with even greater accuracy and with deadly effect. Although the gun was heavier than its predecessor it had a high muzzle velocity that increased the range by some 15,000m. The gun also did not have a standard split-trail carriage, but instead had four outriggers, two of which folded up underneath the barrel during transportation. This ingenious mechanism reduced weight while allowing a 360-degree traverse. These heavy field guns were seen both in the ranks of the Wehrmacht and Waffen-SS, and actually formed the core of SS divisional artillery.

Although the 15cm s FH 18/43 was revolutionary for its time, the gun saw service mainly in Russia. But with the war drawing into a long bloody battle of attrition, more demands were made for further improvements in the s FH 18 class of weapon. Designers were therefore given the task to produce the gun with all-round fire, high-angle fire and a range of at least 18,000m in order to out-range Red Army opposition. Krupp, Skoda and Rheinmetall all produced designs of the 15cm schwere Feldhaubitze 43 or 15cm s FH 43 gun. They even made wooden mock-ups of the design. However, due to the cost and the time that it would take to enter the gun into service the plans were subsequently abandoned.

Another design that was still in the experimental stage during the later phase of the war was for a 15cm long-range shell using a thin metal body enclosing a concrete lining in which metal fragments were embedded. The shell had been specifically designed to be fired from the s FH 18 series, but as the war came to an abrupt end, so did the development of the shell.

The crew of a 10cm s. K18 heavy gun prepares to load. In the Wehrmacht the heavy field guns were composed of the 10cm and 15cm howitzers. The 10cm gun was the most specialised piece of artillery out of the two calibres. It was a long-range weapon intended to attack enemy artillery with counter-battery fire. Many divisions lacked the 10cm battery due to critical shortages of this weapon.

A well camouflaged 15cm gun. In order to conceal it from aerial observation the crew have moved the gun in between trees and attached foliage over the entire weapon including spade trails and the end of the barrel.

A 15cm field howitzer in its elevated position is being prepared for action by the crew. Special metal-lined wicker cases protecting the projectiles have been carefully stacked together to the rear as a ready ammunition station.

The gun leader signals the 15cm gun to be fired by raising his right arm. The gun layer, who aims the gun, can be seen seated to the left of the breech. As the standard heavy field howitzer in the Wehrmacht, the gun was very effective at clearing up heavily concentrated positions to let tanks and infantry pour through unhindered.

A new 15cm field howitzer during the opening phase of the French Campaign in May 1940. Before an armoured strike, artillery crews concentrated on the enemy tanks in the assembly areas, unleashing their firepower where anti-tank units were suspected to be located. Artillery fire was heaviest where Panzers would be unable to operate, but from where they could be engaged effectively.

With total aerial superiority in northern France the crew of this 15cm howitzer have not improvised with camouflage, and remain out in the open in a field with their barrel in an elevated position. Note the mat placed beneath the wheel in order to prevent the gun from sinking.

A battery of 15cm howitzers during the French Campaign. The power of these heavy field guns could hurl its destructive charge nearly 9 miles into the enemy lines.

On the Eastern Front during the winter of 1941 and a 15cm howitzer can be seen in action. The gun has been ideally positioned and blends well with the trees, in spite of the artic conditions. The letter `C` painted in white on the recoil cylinder bracket is the guns designation within the battery.

Here a 15cm gun has just fired off one of its projectiles as the weapon can be seen in full recoil. Various items including propellant cartridge containers and projectile wicker cases are seen neatly placed on the grass, ready to be used at a moments notice.

On the battlefield a 15cm field howitzer is seen in its elevated position. This particular gun was designed to attack targets deeper in the enemy's rear. This included command posts, reserve units, assembly areas, and logistics facilities.

A 15cm gun in action. Much of the transportation of the artillery, especially between 1939 and 1942, was undertaken by animal draught. However, crews preferred tracked vehicles, which enabled them to work more effectively and minimised the distance between artillery and advanced Panzer units.

At a barracks a newly arrived polished and cleaned 15cm howitzer awaits inspection. The gun has pre-war camouflage paint applied. On the two elevating cylinders the letters `A` painted in white indicate the gun's designation within the battery.

Strategically placed in a line of trees is a battery of 15cm howitzers. All the guns are in their elevated position and in action against Soviet targets. The divisional artillery was organised into four battalions, each referred to as an `Abteilung`. Each Abteilung were comprised of three firing batteries with each battery containing four howitzers.

A very well concealed 15cm howitzer on the Eastern Front in 1941. The weapon has been camouflaged with plenty of foliage from the surrounding trees. Of interest is the elevation/range table painted on the left side of the breech where the gun-layer seat is attached.

The crew of a 15cm howitzer in Russia during the summer of 1941. There were 15 crewmembers to each gun, 7 of which are seen here. One of the crewmembers is holding what appears to be a primed projectile, ready for firing. The rammer waits patiently whilst the gunner-layer aims the gun. The battery's supporting NCO can be seen holding a report or map in his hand.

The deafening blast of the 15cm howitzer leaving the barrel can only be imagined by the sight of two crewmembers in this photograph plugging their ears. This particular weapon was capable of firing eight different propellant charges, depending on the range and desired effect on the target.

During the night a 10cm howitzer opens fire on a Russian target. As the projectile leaves the barrel it generates a massive muzzle flash that lights up the night sky.

An interesting photograph showing an unmanned 15cm howitzer during a lull in the fighting on the Eastern Front in 1941. The weapon is yet to see action as the projectiles can still be seen stacked together at the rear. Note the camouflage netting draped over part of the gun and the red and white-striped aiming stake lying on the grass.

An artilleryman poses for the camera in front of a towed 15cm howitzer. The average artilleryman's equipment was basic and consisted of a leather belt, a rifle ammunition pouch, the M1938 gasmask in its metal canister, a field flask, bread bag and the Wehrmacht waterproof Zeltbahn. For personal defence he was normally issued with a K 98k automatic rifle and small arms pistol.

A pause in the fighting on the Eastern Front during the summer of 1942. A 15cm howitzer has been deployed in an open field and the crew have applied lots of heavy foliage to help conceal it from aerial observation. The heat coupled with hard physical work has led to three of the crewmembers to remove their shirts

A 15cm howitzer during a training exercise in the autumn of 1940. Special mats to prevent the gun from sinking into the soft ground have been placed beneath the steel wheels. The steel wheels are the cast-aluminium-type with steel rims issued to horse-drawn artillery units.

Two crewmembers pose for the camera with their howitzer on the Eastern Front in 1941. Mats have been placed beneath the weapon's wheels to prevent the gun from sinking. By avoiding the wheels from sinking it helped with the effects of the gun's accuracy whilst firing.

In June 1940, northern France, a 15 cm heavy field howitzer sits under camouflage netting. This weapon saw extensive use during the Western campaign in 1940 and was used to support not only the advancing troops, but armour as well.

A battery of 10cm howitzers in the summer of 1942 on the Eastern Front. The 10cm howitzer was primarily intended for long-range counter battery fire. However, it was considered too heavy for its intended duties. Efforts were made to develop a lighter gun for this role, but because of cost the 10cm howitzer remained in service until the end of the war.

On the Eastern Front ten of the fifteen-man crew of a 15cm field howitzer prepare for firing during action in the summer of 1941. As one crewman prepares to load a projectile, behind him another waits with the cartridge case. Note the crewman on the right holding the rammer.

A howitzer on the Eastern Front during winter operations. The gun has received a liberal application of camouflage winter whitewash paint. Some of the barrel has clearly not received a proper coating, which obviously suggests it is a rushed job.

A crewman rests on one of the gun trails out in a field somewhere in southern Russia in the summer of 1941. Note the trail spade dug deep into the soft earth. The trail spades were designed to help prevent the full impact of the howitzers recoil after firing and reduce the backward movement of the gun.

The crew of a 15cm howitzer during action in southern Russia in 1942. In spite of the terrain factor in parts of southern Russia the 15cm howitzer provided reliable support, especially in a defensive role.

A crew rest between the gun trails of a 15cm howitzer during a lull in the fighting on the Eastern Front in 1942. The men tuck into their rations before resuming action. Life as an artilleryman could be very physical and the men always took full advantage of the resting periods they had.

A 15cm howitzer during the early winter of 1941. The gun is being prepared for firing and the rammer stands poised to set the projectile into the chamber. Foliage has been applied to part of the weapon, which surprisingly blends well with the surrounding trees.

In the distance plumes of smoke rises skyward, indicating intensive fighting in the area against Soviet forces in 1941. A 15cm howitzer sits beneath a camouflage net training its powerful barrel in the direction of the fighting. Besides concealing the weapon, camouflage nets also served to deny the enemy the ability to identify the type of artillery piece that occupied the position.

A 15cm battery on the Eastern Front in the early winter of 1943. The standard artillery organisation consisted of some eight 15cm s. FH18 howitzers. Each Abteilung comprised of three firing batteries with each battery containing four howitzers.

Chapter Four

Anti-Aircraft Guns

The use of German anti-aircraft artillery or flak guns was primarily used during the war to defend a position against attacking aircraft. The production of the flak guns contained less variety of weaponry than some of the other classes of artillery that were used during the Second World War. Against Poland in September 1939 the Luftwaffe flak gun strength totalled some 8,950 weapons, half of which were smaller than 5cm calibre. By June 1944 this figure had drastically increased to a total of 45,550 guns, 30,463 of which were light weapons. By this period of the war flak gun crews were already using a variety of weapons to combat not only aerial attacks but ground targets as well. The anti-aircraft guns were primarily designed to deliver a barrage of exploding shells against enemy aircraft. The effectiveness of such flak fire generally required firing literally thousands of rounds of ammunition in order to prevent the enemy aircraft from completing their mission successfully. The success of the flak gun in Poland, the Western campaign in 1940 and then the battles on the Eastern Front in 1941, saw large increases in the number of flak units. During 1942-43 panzergrenadier regiments received regimental light flak companies. These included self-propelled 3.7cm medium flak guns and quadruple 2cm guns.

By late 1943 and early 1944, both the Wehrmacht and Waffen-SS mechanised formations had become very well equipped with flak guns. Apart from a five-battery motorised flak battalion, divisions also had additional flak platoons and companies in their Panzergrenadier, Panzer and artillery regiments. A typical SS Panzer division in 1944 for instance was authorised with some 80 towed and 40 self-propelled 2cm guns, six 2cm quadruple weapons, nine 3.7cm guns and 12 heavy 8.8cm flak weapons.

The first flak gun to be mass produced and to see active service during the war was the 2cm Flugabwehrkanone 30 or 2cm Flak 30. In 1935 the 2cm Flak 30 was taken into use by the Luftwaffe as a field-service flak weapon and was seen four years later in action in Poland. The weapon had a box magazine and was recoil operated. Two triggers were used; the left trigger gave automatic fire whilst the right gave single shots. The gun was mounted on a mobile trailer that could be easily towed by almost any vehicle. It had a sight, a reflector mirror with a mechanical course-and-speed calculator. The Flak 30 was very basic in design. It was relatively easy to use and remained in service throughout the war, in spite of it being replaced by the Flak 38.

The 2cm Flugabwehrkanone 38 or 2cm Flak 38 (Erika) was another popular weapon seen during the outbreak of war in 1939. It had a very good performance and by the end of the war there had been some 17,589 of them in use. Although used in a primary anti-aircraft role, it was also used as a light support weapon, and was supplied not only to the Luftwaffe, but to the Navy, Wehrmacht and Waffen-SS as well. The gun was almost identical to the earlier Flak 30 model with the same mounting and equipment, but there were slight variations in models depending on their task and within the units they served. There was the Flakvierling 38 for instance that was produced in late 1940. This was a quadruple arrangement of guns on a platform and carriage similar to that of the single gun, but strengthened and enlarged. They were mounted on various platforms including half-tracked and other wheeled vehicles. They were also used on top of flak towers and other strategically important defensive positions, as well as being fitted to sea vessels.

Another flak gun to be manufactured, but to see limited service, was the 3.7cm Flugabwehrkanone 36 und 37 or 3.7cm Flak 36 and 37 (Westerwald). This Flak gun was little more than an improved version of that used with the 2cm Flak guns and consisted of a two-wheeled trailer that carried a three-legged mounting. The Flak 36 became the standard light anti-aircraft weapon. When an improved mechanical sight was fitted the gun was changed to Flak 37. However, only a limited number of these weapons were converted.

Another flak to be produced in limited supply was the 3.7cm Flugabwehrkanone 43 or the 3.7cm Flak 43 (Schwarzwald). This weapon was slightly fitted with a longer barrel than the Flak 36. The mounting of the gun was on a three-legged platform upon which the gun revolved. Shortly after its introduction a two-barrelled version was developed known as the Flakwilling 43. This consisted of a heavier stronger mounting that was carried on two-wheel bogies. The gun was a very effective weapon but only 390 of them were ever built.

Whilst these flak guns were being produced the Germans were well aware of the gap in size between the maximum effective ceiling of the light weapons and the minimum of the heavy guns. As a consequence Rheinmetall developed a 5cm flak gun. By the time the Wehrmacht had unleashed its forces against the Russians in June 1941, they were already in service. The gun was a 5cm Flugabwehrkanone 41 or 5cm Flak 41. Although they saw service with the Luftwaffe, they were limited in numbers because they were unstable when fired and the sight was too complicated to use along with a poor calculating mechanism.

Of all the flak guns that were introduced into service one of the best-known and reliable weapons was the 8.8cm Flugabwehrkanone 18, 36 und 37 or 8.8cm Flak 18, 36 and 37. This mighty anti-aircraft gun was known by the Allied troops as the `88`. It was a very deadly and effective piece of weaponry and scored sizable hits both in an anti-aircraft role and against ground targets as well. The first of the 8.8cm guns to enter service was the Flak 18 in 1933. Three years later in 1936 the Flak 36 was developed. Just before the war the Flak 37 was introduced. All three versions were extensively used during the war by the Luftwaffe, Wehrmacht and later the Waffen-SS. These three services also used another new 8.8cm Flak gun. It was known as the 8.8cm Flugabwehrkanone 41 or 8.8cm Flak 41 (Eisenerz) and was built specifically for a duel role and possessed a genuine anti-tank capability. Its longer 71-calibre barrel gave it an increased muzzle velocity and better penetration. In service it proved robust, reliable, and icontinued in production until the end of the war.

The most famous German anti-aircraft gun of World War II was the heavy flak 8.8cm. The gun was bolted on a cruciform platform from which it fired with outriggers extended. Here in this photograph, taken in 1941 in Russia, a well-camouflaged 8.8cm Flak gun with its barrel in an elevated position. Note the gun trailer heavily camouflaged as well.

A 2cm flak gun scouring the sky for enemy aircraft during the first part of the invasion of Russia in June 1941. The 2cm gun was the first flak gun to see active service both in Wehrmacht and Waffen-SS units.

In a field on a very warm summers day on the Eastern Front and the crew of an 8.8cm Flak gun prepares for a fire-mission. Note, although the crew are shirtless they are still wearing their helmets for protection.

A battery of flak 8.8cm guns open fire during a night time Soviet aerial attack on German positions in the summer of 1942 near Kharkov. Note the guns' limbers positioned nearby. The limbers were normally positioned like this in order for the crews to rapidly limber-up and re-position the gun.

An 8.8cm flak gun in its full-elevated position is poised for action against enemy aircraft. The barrel of the gun has victory markings painted in white. These were known as barrel kill rings and German military units painted them on most of their guns or vehicles that had destroyed enemy aircraft, vehicles, or other targets.

A Wehrmacht flak crew train their 2cm flak gun on a suspected aerial target in southern Russia in 1941. The gun was mounted on a simple three-legged platform upon which the gun revolved, and the two-wheeled trailer carried it into action.

As an 8.8cm gun hurls its projectile into the air a red signal flag is raised by the Luftwaffe battery officer issuing orders to halt the firing, which signified the end of the air raid or threat of aerial attack in the area.

A well camouflaged 8.8cm flak gun in action by a Wehrmacht flak unit during operations in Army Group Centre in Russia in the summer of 1941. The gun's high velocity and flat trajectory made it very accurate and effective in both an anti-aircraft and anti-tank role.

The crew of a 2cm Luftwaffe Flak gun in a makeshift position on the Russian Northern Front in the autumn of 1941. The gun was a very effective weapon and had a fire rate of 120 – 280 rounds per minute.

A 2cm flak gun and its Luftwaffe crew during operations in France in early June 1940. Once the gun was levelled by three adjustable feet, the gun layer could then climb into the seat and the gun was ready for action. Here the gun layer can be seen looking through the gun sight, whilst behind him another crewman stands holding an optical range finder.

Luftwaffe crews with their 3.7cm Flak guns on a training exercise. The gun itself was no more than an enlarged version of the 2cm flak gun with a two-wheel trailer. The gun was mounted on cruciform platform where it could fire a projectile to a vertical height of 4,785m.

The Wehrmacht crew of an 8.8cm Flak gun pose for the camera during the initial stages of `Barbarossa`, the code-name for the German invasion of Russia in June 1941.

A 2cm light flak gun with its Luftwaffe battery in 1940. By this period of the war the Germans began improvising both the 2cm and 3.7cm flak gun and utilising a number of tracked and commercial vehicles to carry the flak guns into battle.

Mounted on its cruciform platform the 2cm flak gun is trained across a field somewhere on the Eastern Front in 1941. The weapon's fire rate was more than capable of dealing with attacking enemy troop concentrations.

A 2cm flak gun in action. Although these light anti-aircraft guns were used extensively to deal with the regenerated threat of the Soviet Air Force, the recurring appearance of heavier enemy armour compelled many flak crews to divert their attention from the air and support their own infantry and armour on the ground in an anti-tank role

A Luftwaffe flak position overlooking a river on the side of a hill. Strong anti-aircraft defences only came into prominence in September 1941, as the Soviet Air Force started to inflict heavy casualties on German divisions.

Some searchlights that have been concealed beneath tarpaulin prior to their transportation to a Luftwaffe flak battery. The searchlights were used in order to detect both ground and aerial targets and allow flak crews to aim their weapons more accurately at the target.

An 8.8cm flak battery on the Eastern Front in 1942. As the Soviet Air Force increased in size and inflicted ever-greater casualties on German positions, so the need for more 8.8cm flak guns to try and counter the growing threat.

An 8.8cm flak gun in a position overlooking a river in Russia in 1942. This flak gun was used in two roles, one as a mobile heavy anti-aircraft battery, and also in a more static role for the defence of Germany. In this latter role the guns were arranged into large batteries, directed by a single controller, and were moved only rarely.

An unmanned 2cm flak gun on a firing platform installation near what appears to be a German barracks. The gun became the primary light anti-aircraft gun used by the Wehrmacht and Waffen-SS.

A typical 2cm flak detachment consisted of seven men, although fewer often crewed the flak installations. Here in this photograph is almost a full compliment of the crew posing for the camera.

A battery of 3.7cm flak guns on their two-wheeled trailers during the early phase of the campaign in Russia. The guns are concealed beneath tarpaulins not only to camouflage the weapons, but also to protect them against dust and dirt.

A 3.7cm flak gun on an installation protecting a busy shipping lane from aerial attack. The mounting of the gun is on a cruciform platform, and transported on a two-wheeled limber, which can be seen in this photograph.

The crew of a 2cm flak gun in Germany protecting a river estuary during the summer of 1941. Note the crewman using an optical range finder to correct fire for the flak battery. Should rounds fall short or over the target, his task was to advise the flak aimer on the corrections needed for the battery to hit the target.

Two Luftwaffe crewmen belonging to a 2cm flak gun battery tuck into their rations during a rest from defence duties in Germany in 1941. The 2cm flak gun was suitable for attacking low flying aircraft, and not high altitude precision bombers that would make their debut in great numbers a year later over Germany.

A Luftwaffe 2cm flak 30 crew preparing for a fire mission against an enemy target during the winter of 1941 in Germany. The projectiles used by this weapon were airburst shells. The airburst shells were favoured for their anti-personnel capabilities against troops in cover. The explosive force of a 2cm H.E. shell was small, about the same as a hand grenade.

The gunner has elevated his flak gun after sighting aircraft in the area. Three crewmen can be seen using the optical range finder suggesting aerial activity maybe relatively on large-scale.

A battery of 8.8cm flak guns in their specially constructed installations in southern Russia in 1942. These guns are positioned for an air-defence role and were lethal weapons to enemy aircraft.

A Luftwaffe 2cm Flak crew rest during a lull in the fighting. The number of guns assigned to light flak batteries varied through the war, but was typically twelve 2cm and/or 3.7cm guns in four platoons.

Out in North Africa in 1942, and a Luftwaffe 3.7cm flak gun crew have elevated the barrel in preparation for firing at an enemy target. Note the nineteen kill rings painted in white on the barrel.

The `88` was arguably the most effective anti-aircraft and anti-tank gun used in both the North African and Russian campaigns. Where the terrain was often flat and open it allowed the long-range performance of the gun to be decisive.

This flak gun is being used in a ground role against British forces in North Africa in 1942. The position is well dug in and allows the gun to be protected and concealed with surrounding earth and sandbags.

Here a battery of 8.8cm flak guns open fire against enemy aircraft during a night-time air raid. As early as 1939 the Luftwaffe had been in charge of anti-aircraft defences instead of the Wehrmacht.

A Luftwaffe battery officer using a field telephone during operations in Russia in 1941. Note his binoculars and container rest. The battery officer was responsible for relaying orders to the gun leaders and supervising the daily running of the crews and the guns themselves.

The Luftwaffe crew of an 8.8cm flak gun in action on the Eastern Front in 1942. The `88` could actually be fired while mounted on its limbers, but the instability affected the accuracy and the rate of fire.

A Luftwaffe search light company on the Eastern Front in 1942. Although these searchlights were used mainly for aerial duties, locating enemy aircraft for flak batteries, they were also used for ground operations as well.

An 8.8cm Luftwaffe flak gun mounted on its limber being towed in 1943. Nearby is a long-range optical range finder. Normally the `88` was served by a 10-man crew plus a halftrack driver, who was considered part of the crew.

On a training exercise somewhere in Germany in the winter of 1940, two 2cm flak 30 guns open fire on their two-wheeled trailer. These guns rarely fired from their trailer platforms due to the instability and inaccuracy of firing.

A crewman of an Sd.Kfz.10/4 halftrack sits in front of his vehicle during winter operations on the Eastern Front in 1944. The gun mounted on top of the halftrack is a 2cm Flak 30, which can be identified by the shape of its shield and the configuration of its tube. Note the unusual white wash camouflage pattern on the gun shield.

Taken in the winter of 1944 is a Waffen-SS flak crew with their Sd.Kfz.10/4 halftrack with a 2cm Flak 30 gun mounted on the back. During the war the Waffen-SS raised 49 anti-aircraft battalions and 22 independent companies.

A Waffen-SS halftrack with a 2cm Flak gun mounted on the back during the winter on the Eastern Front in 1944. The sides of the vehicle are folded up with additional magazine cases attached. These sides could be folded down to allow extra space on board the halftrack for the flak crew. Note what appears to be kill markings painted on the vehicles fender.

This photograph was taken in southern Poland in the summer of 1944. It shows a halftrack with a quadruple barrelled self-propelled flak gun on the back. This gun could unleash a hurricane of fire and was able to discharge 1800 rounds per minute from all four of its barrels

A Waffen-SS halftrack armed with a 2cm quadruple self-propelled flak gun during operations in 1944. The weapon could engage not only air targets but ground ones as well. With the folding sides down the gun was very adaptable and could traverse 360 degrees, making it a very lethal weapon of war.

An 8.8cm Flak gun in action firing at an aerial target during a night-time attack on the Eastern Front. To help stem the serious losses sustained by the air offensive, thousands of flak guns were rushed into service and made widely available to all branches of the armed services, including home defence units.

A white-washed 8.8cm flak gun being used against a ground target during the winter of 1943 in Russia. The dismounted limber can be seen next to the flak gun, just as a precautionary measure that the crew need to hastily re-position the gun. Note the unhampered access to the ammunition stockpile.

A flak crew at a training ground celebrating Christmas Day in western Russia in 1941 with a crate of well-earned alcoholic beverages. Note the lack of winter clothing worn by the crew during this first winter period on the Eastern Front.

A battery of 8.8cm flak guns during a night-time attack on the Eastern Front. The gun has been installed into a deliberately constructed position of planks and timber brick and concrete. Such positions usually had canvas covers concealing the gun and its equipment. Note the entrance to the specially adapted bunker system for the crews sleeping quarters.

Reichsmarschall Herman Goring, commander-in-Chief of the Luftwaffe, inspects an 8.8cm flak gun with other commanding officers after the victory in France in 1940.

Chapter Five

Anti-Tank Guns

One of the most important defensive and offensive tactics for the Wehrmacht during the war was its ability to counter enemy armour on the battlefield. For this reason the Germans were determined to find a mobile weapon capable of firing solid shot at high velocity so that it could easily penetrate the armour of enemy tanks. As early as 1928 the first viable German anti-tank gun had been designed. It emerged as the 3.7cm Panzerabwehrkanone L/45. The gun was a relatively low-calibre, mobile weapon capable of firing solid shot at high velocity. It was light and easy to conceal and could penetrate the armour of almost any tank then in service. By 1935 a modified version of the anti-tank weapon was introduced. It was the 3.7cm Panzerabwehrkanone 35/36 or 3.7cm Pak 36. The gun was very similar to the original design and was carried on a two-wheel split-trail carriage of tubular construction with a small-sloped splinter shield. The Pak 36 emerged as the first anti-tank weapon to serve in both the Wehrmacht and Waffen-SS.

When the Wehrmacht unleashed its mighty forces against Poland in September 1939 the use of the anti-tank gun was rather limited against an opponent who had inadequate tank capability. However, by the time they attacked the Low Countries and France in 1940 the war showed them that on occasion, a number of guns were needed to fight tanks, and this included the extensive use of the Pak 36. It was not until the battles on the Western Front that the Wehrmacht soon came to appreciate the tactical limitations of the Pak 36 against British and French armour. Consequently, following the German victory over France, commanders concluded that the Wehrmacht needed a heavier anti-tank gun. A year later whilst fighting in the vast expanses of the Soviet Union it reconfirmed this fear of the growing obsolescence of the Pak 36.

However, by 1941 the Germans had already introduced an anti-tank gun to replace the Pak 36. It was available by the end of 1940 and was known as the 5cm Panzerabwehrkanone 38 or 5cm Pak 38. The gun itself was of conventional design, fitted with a muzzlebrake and semi automatic breech. The carriage had a split trail with tubular legs and solid-tyre disc wheels. Although initially the Luftwaffe used the Pak 38, it was soon found in the ranks of the Wehrmacht. In fact, the gun was destined to become the most widely used anti-tank gun by the Waffen-SS. But once again on the Eastern Front anti-tank gunners soon realised that a more powerful gun would be needed to combat the heavier Red Army tanks.

In late 1941 a new anti-tank gun reached Wehrmacht and Waffen-SS troops in Russia. It was the 7.5cm Panzerabwehrkanone 40 or 7.5cm Pak 40 (Hünengrab). The gun was virtually an enlarged version of the Pak 38, using the similar split-trail and a double skinned splinter shield. It became the standard anti-tank gun of the war and because it was relatively cheap to produce it remained in production until 1945. The gun had undoubtedly arrived in Russia at the right time. During the terrible arctic conditions of 1941 and early 1942, the Germans had found themselves thinly stretched across the Eastern Front against an enemy that was undefeated. It was for this reason that the new anti-tank gun was so desperately needed. When the gun crews received batches of the first Pak 40`s they were almost immediately inserted into line for action. Within hours the new anti-tank weapons were proving their worth on the battlefield. Its effectiveness made the gun very popular, but there were never enough Pak 40 guns to meet the ever-increasing demand in the East. Throughout its life on the battlefield the Pak 40 was a powerful and deadly weapon, especially in the hands of well-trained anti-tank gunners. However, because of its weight this led to instances where gun crews reluctantly abandoned their precious Pak 40 because they could not manhandle them in bad ground conditions caused by the winter snow and spring thaw.

Whilst the Pak 40 continued to do sterling service in Russia, there was still the need to further produce anti-tank guns to confront the ever increasing heavy Soviet tanks. It was for this reason that yet another Pak gun entered service. It was known as the 7.5cm Panzerabwehrkanone 41 or 7.5cm Pak 41. The few guns that were produced were largely issued to special duty units, but production was soon halted due to the restrictions placed on the use of tungsten.

During this period of the war a number of other Pak guns were introduced during the Russian campaign and this included the use of captured French and Soviet guns. Among these was the deployment of the 7.5cm Panzerabwehrkanone 97/38 or 7.5cm Pak 97/38. This French built gun model of 1897 had its barrel removed from their original field mountings and fitted with a Pak 38 carriage.

Another gun to see extensive service with the Germans, especially during the earlier part of the war in Russia was the vast captured stocks of the standard Soviet field gun, the 76.2mm 1936 and the 7.62cm 1939 models. These weapons were immediately put into German use and a number of them were redesigned as antitank guns. They were known as the 7.62cm Panzerabwehrkanone 36r or 7.62cm Pak 36r and the 7.62cm Panzerabwehrkanone 39r or 7.62cm Pak 39r. Both these guns were a very successful and efficient weapon, but still were unable to properly compete against the nation that had developed them.

Although the captured Soviet guns became one of the best anti-tank weapons used during the war, the Germans realised by 1942 that eventually an even heavier and more potent gun would be required on the battlefield to help prevent the growing might of the Russian tank and its thick armour. During 1943 Krupp designed the 8.8cm Panzerabwehrkanone 43 or 8.8cm Pak 43 (Neuntoter). This became the finest anti-tank gun to enter service in the ranks of the Wehrmacht and Waffen-SS. When it arrived at the front for the first time in 1944, it was capable of knocking out any tank in service during this period of the war. The gun was so efficient and deadly it even proved superior to that of the improvised dual-purpose 8.8cm Flak 41. The powerful long 71-calibre barrel with muzzlebrake could be fired from its firing platform while limbered, though over restricted traverse. But in spite of its very useful tactical capability in which it scored sizable hits against the enemy, the Pak 43 was not cheap, and as a consequence was in short supply.

Despite the ever-increasing production and utilisation of the dual purpose flak guns and captured weapons, there were never enough anti-tank guns to protect the German divisions that were exposed almost daily to the full rigours of enemy warfare. Nonetheless, the Germans continued to fight on with what they had at their disposal and displayed all the skill and élan that made them one of the best fighting formations in the world.

Troops connecting a 3.7cm Pak 35/36 anti-tank gun to a vehicle whilst on exercise in southern Germany in 1937. This weapon was the first anti-tank gun mass produced and saw service in both the Wehrmacht and Waffen-SS.

Wehrmacht troops more than likely on exercise as one of the soldiers can be seen with a white armband. The men are pulling a 3.7cm Pak 35/36 gun up a riverbank. Although the gun only weighed 432kg, it still required eight soldiers or more to pull the weapon up a steep slope.

The crew of a 7.5cm Pak 38 gun, position their gun for firing during the winter of 1943. In service this anti-tank weapon proved very powerful and deadly and became one of the most widely used German anti-tank guns between 1942 and 1944.

A vehicle tows a 7.5cm Pak 97/38 during operations on the Eastern Front. This captured french 7.5cm gun had the barrels of these removed from their original field mountings and fitted into modified 5cm Pak 38 carriages.

Pak 35/36 gunners during the Polish Campaign in September 1939. It was here in Poland that anti-tank crews found that their Pak guns more than adequate for operational needs in the face of relatively modest armoured opposition.

An 8.8cm on its limber being towed by a vehicle. Although the `88` was widely used as an anti-aircraft gun it also possessed a genuine anti-tank capability. On the battlefield it proved a very versatile weapon and continued being used in a dual role until the end of the war.

A 3.7cm Pak 35/36 crew from the SS division `Nord` during operations on the Russian Northern Front in 1941. By the time the Germans attacked Russia Pak 35/36 gunners quickly recognised the growing obsolesce of their weapon, especially against the new T-34 tanks.

An 8.8cm flak gun on the battlefield during the French campaign in 1940. Although the gun has been installed for anti-aircraft defence it is clear by the elevation of the weapon that is also being utilised in a dual anti-tank role.

A Wehrmacht flak crew pose for the camera holding the gun's 8.8cm projectiles. Although the `88` was no doubt an effective gun, it was also skilfully publicised into an all-conquering dual-action super weapon, which certainly it was not.

During a lull in the fighting an 8.8cm Flak gun with fitted shield is being used by a Luftwaffe crew in an anti-tank and anti-aircraft role on the Eastern Front during the summer of 1942.

The crew of an 8.8cm Flak gun take cover behind their gun during an aerial attack in North Africa in 1941. It was here in the North African desert that the `88` became a proven and deadly weapon, both against ground and aerial targets.

An 8.8cm Luftwaffe flak crew are changing a tyre to the gun's two-wheeled limber. Once the gun was positioned for action, the two-wheel limbers would be removed after lowing the platform of the gun by hand winches, which can be seen in this photograph either side of the limber. In an anti-tank role, these limbers would stay relatively close to the gun just in case the weapon was needed to be rapidly re-positioned.

Out in North Africa and an 8.8cm gun is in action against a ground target. A difficulty encountered, especially out in the desert against ground targets, was the smoke and considerable amounts of dust raised by the large muzzle blast of the powerful 8.8cm gun.

A Waffen-SS halftrack tows a 7.5cm Pak 40 along a road in 1944. This anti-tank gun proved its worth in Russia and was more than capable of disabling heavy Soviet tanks. Waffen-SS gunners in particular were able to demonstrate the efficacy of the weapon in action in a number of armoured battles in the East.

A halftrack with a 7.5cm Pak 40 on tow is parked at the roadside during operations in the East in 1944. The gun reached Wehrmacht and Waffen-SS troops in Russia in late 1941, and immediately scored a number of successful engagements against Soviet armour.

Being towed by animal draught during the French campaign in 1940 is a 5cm Pak 38. The Pak 38 was the first anti-tank weapon to be produced as full-sized artillery. Although these anti-tank guns proved deadly against French and British forces, by the time they saw action in Russia a year later, German gunners soon realised they needed a more potent anti-tank gun to counter the growing menace of Soviet armour.

An anti-tank crew with their Pak 38 in 1942. The Pak 38 was well liked among the crews that had the chance to use it in battle. Not only was the weapon effective in combat, but also easy to conceal.

A well concealed 7.5cm Pak 40 gun during a firing operation on the Eastern Front. Some foliage has been applied to the splinter shield and 7.5cm barrel and muzzle break. Note how the gunner is well protected by the shield.

Two anti-tank gunners in action loading their Pak gun during a battle on the Eastern Front in 1944. Although the earli Pak guns proved i worth in combat the Germans had desperately neede a gun with a heavier punch. By 1944 they introduced the Pa 43, which was the finest anti-tank gu to see operationa service during World War Two.

A very well camouflaged Pak 35/36 during the French campaign in 1940. It was during the campaign in the West that German anti-tank gunners encountered Allied heavy tanks and realised that their thick armour proved impervious to the 3.7cm anti-tank rounds.

Chapter Six

Transporting Guns

Preparing artillery for action on the battlefield relied heavily on the various light and heavy armoured vehicles for transportation. Maintaining the momentum of an advance was vital to success and, without transport, the whole advance might stall. It was for this reason that the Germans utilised a variety of horse drawn and armoured vehicles to tow or carry artillery to the forward edge of the battlefield. The various carriages, haulage trailers and towing equipment were a necessity for any force preparing to go into action, allowing it to function in a cohesive and well-defined manner. It was for this reason that the Germans intended making their army an all-mechanised armoured force. However, by the time the Wehrmacht rolled across the frontier into Poland in September 1939 they still absolutely depended upon the horse for over eighty-percent of motive power for towing or carrying artillery pieces.

Even two years later during the invasion of Russia in June 1941, almost three quarters of a million horses alone were used in the opening attack. Although a great number of the horses were used to carry soldiers or transport various supplies to the front, these beasts still towed huge amounts of artillery from one sector of the front to another. The bulk of the artillery was originally intended for horse drawn transport, especially light pieces like the 7.5cm FK 16, FK 18, and FK 38. These were known as a horse-drawn cavalry-accompanying gun. The 10.5cm le FH 18/40 and le FH 18/42 were also designed to be towed by horses. Heavy artillery like the 10cm K18, 15cm s FH 36, 15cm s FH 40, 15cm s FH 18/40, and the 15cm s FH 18/43 were all primarily moved by both animal draught or vehicle traction. The barrel was completely withdrawn from the cradle on to a four-wheel transport wagon, the carriage forming the second load. Both loads normally saw the use of eight-horse teams.

The weight of the artillery pieces and the way in which they had to be transported and positioned in the field, especially the heavier guns like the 15cm calibre artillery, were reasons enough why the guns needed tracked vehicles rather than the horse. Animal draught took much longer to carry the guns to the battlefield. In fact during the Polish campaign the artillery arm had been seriously criticised after the fighting. The artillery batteries had not moved forward quickly enough to give continuing support to the attacking infantry. The slow movement of artillery had seriously impeded the blitzkrieg theory. In fact in Poland it had been the Luftwaffe, not the artillery arm that had devoted the greater part of its resources to supporting the Wehrmacht. General Heinz Guderian, the famous Panzer ace, had concluded that bomber aircraft was to be the blitzkrieg's artillery. But in spite of his thoughts the Luftwaffe did not provide the constant artillery bombardment that the ground troops required. For the immediate needs of battle, the mighty Panzer divisions needed an artillery arm that was composed mainly of vehicle traction. Each Panzer division had three battalions of artillery. The heavy battalion had twelve 15cm guns (three batteries, each with four guns). The two light artillery battalions each had twelve 10.5cm guns. These artillery battalions desperately needed to be moved quickly and efficiently alongside the Panzer divisions, and not hindered by slow moving horse drawn transport. It was therefore a priority for the artillery arm to be supplied with tracked vehicles. These specially adapted vehicles were able to move across country quicker, and tow an intact 15cm gun without wasting valuable time by breaking it down into two loads. The artillery crew could all sit in relative comfort inside the halftrack, instead of struggling along riding on a horse, cavalry drawn wagons, caissons or limbers.

In order to support the doctrine of blitzkrieg, the Germans designed several types of half tracked tractors, which were classified by the weight of their towed load. Altogether there were seven types of half-track that would all be utilised in towing and mounting various artillery guns. This included anti-aircraft and anti-tank weaponry.

The Sd.Kfz.2 was the first halftrack to be used extensively to tow artillery. This vehicle was specially designed to haul special lightweight artillery such as the 7.5cm and 10.5cm I.G 40 guns. The next half-track was the Sd.Kfz.6. This vehicle was a personnel carrier and towed guns like the 10.5cm le. FH 18. Later it was used to haul the 8.8cm PaK 43 or PaK 43/41. A variation mounted a 3.7cm Flak 36/37, whilst another mounted a captured Soviet 7.62cm gun. Another half-track was the Sd.Kfz.7. This was an 8-ton prime mover and mainly hauled 8.8cm Flak guns, as well as the 10cm s. K 18 and 15cm s FH 18. Variations mounted a 2cm Flakvierling 38, or a 3.7cm Flak 37 or 43. After the production of the Sd.Kfz.7 came the Sd.Kfz.8. This was an even larger vehicle that weighed some 12-tons. It was designed to tow heavier artillery such as the 17cm s. K 18, 21cm Morser 18 and 10.5cm Flak 39. The Sd.Kfz.9 was also designed to tow heavy artillery components including the 60cm Morser `Karl`. A small number of these vehicles were converted to mobile Flak guns by adding armour, ammunition stowage and a shielded 8.8cm Flak 36. A much smaller half-track, the Sd.Kfz.10 was used to haul light ordnance such as the 2cm Flak 30 or 38, 3.7cm Pak 36, 5cm Pak 38 and 7.5cm le. IG 18. It was also used to mount a 2cm Flak 30 or Flak 38. Another half-track used to tow light and medium ordnance was Sd.Kfz.11. This 3-ton vehicle towed the 2cm Flakvierling 38, 3.7cm Flak 37 or 43,

7.5cm Pak 40, 10.5cm Le.FH 18, 15cm s. IG 33, 15cm Nebelwerfer 41 and 21cm Nebelwerfer 42. A semi-armoured version mounted a 2cm Flak 38.

Another halftrack used to tow a variety of weaponry, but not to the extent of the artillery prime movers, was the Sd.Kfz.251 medium armoured personnel carrier. These half-tracks towed light and medium ordnance and on rare occasions were seen pulling 8.8cm Flak guns. These vehicles were also used in the artillery batteries for observation.

The half-track vehicle transformed the fighting quality of the artillery batteries and enabled gun crews to support the advancing armoured spearheads with less difficulty. However, it was not just tracked vehicles that increased the efficiency of transport to the battlefield. Among other forms of transportation used by the artillery arm was the wide use of the railway network, especially on the Eastern Front. Both wide-gauge and narrow gauge railway lines transported artillery. The specially built flatcars and platforms allowed loads to be entrained or detrained quickly and easily.

Another form of transportation used by the Wehrmacht was specially built heavy-duty tracked artillery tractors that were specifically used for towing super heavy guns. Because the very big guns were broken down into a number of parts these vehicles were designed to transport the various loads to the firing position. One particular gun could be broken down into six loads and consisted of the barrel, the top carriage, the lower carriage, the front platform, rear platform and the turn table.

An SS.Leibstandarte flak crew pose for the camera with their concealed 2cm Flak gun mounted on a two-wheeled trailer. The gun is being towed by a halftrack, more than likely an Sd.Kfz.10 or Sd.Kfz.11, which were both designed to tow light ordnance.

A 2cm Flak crew belonging to the SS.Leibstandarte during operations in France in 1940. The flak gun is being towed by a support vehicle, which were used extensively in the Wehrmacht, Waffen-SS and Luftwaffe to tow and transport ordnance to the battlefield.

A halftrack wades across a river during the summer of 1942 in Russia. The vehicle is towing an ammunition trailer for either a 2cm or 3.7cm flak gun. Field modifications for this vehicle also saw the 3.7cm and 5cm Pak mounted on the back.

In the Balkans in April 1941 and a halftrack has halted on a road. The vehicle is towing a 10.5cm howitzer, which is being carried on a specially adapted two-wheeled trailer. This special trailer is being used in order to prevent the rapid wear and tear of the gun's wheels, which were originally designed to be towed by animal draught.

The crew of a 5cm Pak 38 moves its piece toward a pontoon bridge during operations in southern Russia in 1942. This anti-tank gun was intended to be towed by a light truck or an Sd.Kfz.10 halftrack.

Here a 15cm howitzer is being towed by horses. The 15cm gun was broken down into two loads, each drawn by six horses. In this photograph the carriage and mounting are seen with equipement secured to the gun trails. The gun's tube and breech were transported on a special four-wheeled wagon.

Two crewmembers clean one of the artillery battery's limbers. The limber itself was basically a two-wheeled cart with an axle, surmounted by a framework for holding an ammunition chest. It was also used to seat two or even three cannoneers, depending on the distances they had to travel.

Here the gun tube and breech of the 15cm howitzer are seen on a transport wagon onboard a specially adapted wide-gauge flat bed railway car. In order for these transport wagons to be moved by train, special loading platforms had been constructed. This allowed the loads to be entrained and detrained quickly.

A 15cm howitzer is being towed by horse drawn transport on the Eastern Front in 1941. The Wehrmacht were dependant on nearly 1,000,000 horses in Russia, all of them used for transportation of some kind. However, some 1000 horses died each day on average. Consequently, a vast amount of organisation was required for the rapid replacement of these animals, and this fell to the already overstretched support services.

A horse drawn artillery Abteilung has halted on a Russian road in 1941 with their towed guns. An average artillery regiment in 1941 was authorised with some 2,500 troops and 2,274 horses. The latter of which drew over 200 wagons and artillery caissons. The majority of the artillery was horse-drawn.

A battery moves forward to the next firing position with horses and crew struggling to move all the equipement across a field. Many crews with their horse drawn transport regularly had great difficulties moving their guns, especially in Russia during the winter periods when rain turned the roads into a quagmire.

Halftrack vehicles are towing well-camouflaged 15cm howitzers towards the frontline in Russia in 1942. Although the guns are well concealed from aerial detection, the dust that that the carriages and vehicles throw into the air could easily be identified from a passing aircraft.

A halftrack tows a 15cm howitzer along a road during the Western Campaign in 1940. It was the Sd.Kfz.7 prime mover that was designed to transport the 15cm s. FH 18 along with the 8.8cm flak, and the 10cm s. K 18 gun.

Despite the power of horses, this crew has to provide assistance as the team strains to drag the gun and limber up a slope. The exertion put on some horses were tremendous, with some of them actually dieing of heart attacks.

The view in this photograph depicts the 15cm howitzer being towed by an 8-ton Sd.Kfz.7 half-track. By 1942 the need for tracked vehicles to transport the guns to the forward edge of the battlefield were in ever increasing demand.

The crew of a 15cm howitzer in the process of readying their weapon for transport. For this process the howitzer is backed up to the carriage, where the gun tube and breech are slid into the mount using a block-and-tackle.

A crewman of a 15cm howitzer poses for the camera during the first summer in Russia in 1941. A stationary Sd.Kfz.7 half-track is towing the gun along a typical Russian dirt road. Note the amount of supplies stored in the vehicle.

A half-track towing a 10.5cm howitzer with a full compliment of crew negotiates uneven terrain during an artillery regiment's drive through central Russia in 1941.

At a Luftwaffe barracks in Germany and ground personnel can be seen with 2cm Flak guns dismounted to ground platform, and a two-wheeled trailer. The trailer was highly mobile and could be fitted to almost any vehicle. It could be easily attached by simply inserting the shackle pin.

During the campaign in the West a halftrack can be seen towing an 8.8cm flak gun past a damaged French house in May 1940. It was after the battle of France that the Germans became even more aware of the significance of providing half-track transportation to the artillery and flak regiments.

A halftrack tows a Mörser to another position on the Eastern Front in 1941. The vehicle is marked as belonging to the 24.Panzer-Division. It was this Panzer division which was destroyed at Stalingrad a year later.

Moving along a road in Russia in 1943 is a halftrack with a mounted 2cm Flak gun. This 1-ton halftrack was also designed to tow light ordnance, which included the 2cm Flak 30 or 3.7cm Pak 36, 5cm Pak 38 and 7.5cm le. IG 18.

An Sd.Kfz.7 halftrack towing a 15cm howitzer has halted along a muddy road after one of the gun carriage wheels has become stuck. In Russia bad terrain was a constant problem for transportation. The appalling mud, coupled with mechanical breakdowns and fierce resistance, caused frequent delays for the Germans who had travelled long distances on board these vehicles.

One of the quickest and easiest forms of transportation across the vast wastelands of the Soviet Union was by railway. Here in this photograph a Luftwaffe flak crew prepare to load an 8.8cm flak gun on board a railway flatcar.

A halftrack towing a 15cm howitzer moves along a typical Russian road during the summer of 1943. A halftrack vehicle caused far less damage to a road than a fully tracked vehicle when moving across country. The half-tracks not only towed artillery or were modified to carry flak guns, but also transformed the fighting quality of the armoured divisions.

A Luftwaffe halftrack has halted next to a fully equipped 8.8cm Flak gun with shield during operations on the Eastern Front in 1942. The carriage was on a cruciform platform on two-wheeled limbers that could be removed after lowering the platform by hand winches.

Watched by inquisitive children is a column of parked halftracks towing 8.8cm flak gun limbers and Luftwaffe support vehicles in France 1940. The halftrack performed a variety of missions in transporting artillery and flak guns to the battlefield, and by 1941 became an integral element of the Wehrmacht armoury.

Two photographs taken of the same halftrack on a training exercise showing the versatility of the vehicle across terrain whilst towing a 10.5cm howitzer. Because these vehicles often supported the armoured drive whilst towing artillery or flak guns they needed to be fast and able to cross some of the most difficult terrain while transporting weapons to the forward edge of the battlefield. The terrain on the Eastern Front would soon test these halftracks to the end of their endurance, sometimes with fatal consequences.

An artillery battery stretches along a field, in a photograph taken during the winter thaw in Russia in March 1942. Horses with attached limbers tow the 10.5cm howitzers across the frozen terrain to the next firing position.

A Waffen-SS armoured transport vehicle laden with a local security patrol from the `Das Reich` division as they pass through a village during its drive towards Moscow in September 1941. Artillery units were expected to provide their own local security defence; infantry units were not normally detailed to protect them.

Wide gauge railway cars are laden with artillery and equipment bound for another part of the Eastern Front in 1942. Beside the special low-level platform are a number of sacks of horse fodder and bales of hay for the horses.

Here horse drawn transport struggles across a muddy field as it tows 10.5cm howitzers, followed by artillerymen on foot. This artillery battery belongs to the SS.Polizei-Division, which saw action on the Leningrad Front in October 1941. Because the Polizei division was regarded as a second rate SS division, it was allotted fewer motorised vehicles than normal, so consequently the majority of its transportation was undertaken by animal draught.

A long column of horse drawn transport moves wearily along a congested muddy road during the SS.Polizei-Division's advance toward the Leningrad Front in September and October 1941. Note the motorcyclist and helping soldiers trying to extract a motorcycle combination from the mud.

The arctic conditions in Russia often made transportation of artillery slow and sometimes perilous. In this photograph a 10.5cm howitzer has slid off the icy road, halting the advance. The steel-rimmed wheels offered no traction on ice or wet and hard surfaces.

Narrow gauge railways were used extensively by the Germans to transport armour and equipment quickly and effectively without the need to travel great distances, which caused persistent wear and tear on the vehicles. In this photograph a battery of 10.5cm howitzers have been loaded on board a narrow gauge train, nicknamed `Flitzkopp`.

A nice view of a 10.5cm howitzer on board a narrow gauge railway car destined for the Russian front lines of Army Group North in 1941. The gun crew are wearing mosquito head-nets to protect themselves against these blood-sucking insects that plagued the forests and swamps around Luga.

A 3.7cm Pak 35/36 gun in June 1940 undergoing what appears to be some repairs by a mobile repair depot. The Pak 36 was a highly mobile weapon. It possessed rubber-tyre wheels, a torsion bar sprung carriage, and could be easily attached to a multitude of transport vehicles.

A halftrack towing what appears to be the components of a gun. The halftrack was primarily designed for decent road speed and efficient flotation in cross-country driving. This ensured that when transporting guns from one position to another it arrived quickly enough to help maintain the advanced armoured spearhead.

Chapter Seven

Super Heavy Guns

When rearmament began the Germans decided to design and develop a series of super heavy guns. These large guns built in a gun mounted mortar (Mörser) style were primarily designed for high-elevation, long-range, counter-battery fire. One of the first of these guns to see its debut during the war was the 17cm Kanone 18 in Mörserlafette or 17cm K 18 in Mrs Laf (Matterhorn). This gun was introduced in 1941 to replace the 15cm weapons, which by then had shown their performance to be insufficient on the battlefield. The 17-ton gun was a long range, counter-battery gun with its carriage designed to allow high elevation. The carriage itself included a sophisticated dual-recoil system where the platform could be lowered to the ground whilst going into action. The weight of the entire gun system was then transferred to the platform by jacking down three castor wheels, which in turn lifted the gun wheels from the ground. This allowed the gun to be rotated through 360 degrees and be fired with full recoil without making the platform unstable. The 17cm K 18 Mörser proved to be one of the best guns in service and had an impressive range, but it was never a common weapon.

Another very large impressive artillery piece to see active service during the war was the Lange 21cm Mörser 18 or 21cm Mrs 18 (Brümmbar). It utilised the same carriage as the 17cm K 18, but in service its range was significantly less than its smaller sister. The gun was regarded as a good weapon but not good enough to warrant volume production, especially as the 17cm K 18 had almost twice its range. As a consequence production ceased in 1942, and designers concentrated on 24cm weapons instead.

The first 24cm gun to be introduced into limited service was the 24cm Kanone L/46 or 24cm K L/46. The general design of the gun was very similar to a scaled-up version of the 15cm K 39. Only a few of these large guns were ever built and none of them survived the war.

The next 24cm gun to be introduced was the 24cm Kanone 3 or 24cm K 3 (Petersdorf). This 83-ton weapon was massive and because of its size could only be transported in six loads. The transport system was regarded as cumbersome, and the fact that it took 25-crew almost 90-minutes to get the weapon ready for action was more than enough reason for it not being practical in terms of manpower and time.

A gun very similar to that of the 24cm K 3 was the 35.5cm Haubitze M1 or 35.5cm H M1. The weapon was introduced into service in 1939 and could also be broken down into six loads. Six 18-ton three-quarter tracked artillery tractors transported the load. On arrival at the front the crew took about two hours to assemble the gun. The weapon's elevating gear and the ammunition hoist were operated by electric power from a generator. The gun fired a standard high explosive projectile weighing over half a ton with a range of some 20,000 metres.

Another super heavy gun that was introduced into service was the railway gun. Although the Germans never extensively used the railway gun they nonetheless saw it as a useful addition to coastal defences, and the fact that it could be used at convenient rail centres and rapidly deployed to a threatened sector of the front. One of the first railway guns to enter service was the 21cm K 12 V (E). This gun with its exceptionally long 109.25ft barrel was fitted to a simple box-girder structure carried on two sub frames that were mounted on double bogies. The front sub frame was on ten-wheels and the rear on two eight-wheel bogies. Altogether the weapon weighed a staggering 313-tons. Only two of these guns were ever issued to service in the summer of 1940 and were used to fire their 107.50kg projectiles across the Channel.

Other railway guns also saw service in a similar role, but again in limited supply. These included the 24cm Kanone in Eisenbahnlafette `Theodor Bruno` or 24cm Th Br K (E). There was the 24cm Kanone in Eisenbahnlafette `Theodor` or 24cm Theodor K (E). Another of these massive weapons was the 28cm Kanone in Eisenbahnlafette `Kurz Bruno` or 28cm Kz Br K (E). This was followed by 28cm Kanone in Eisenbahnlafette `schwere Bruno` or the 28cm s Br K (E) and 28cm Kanone in Eisenbahnlafette `Bruno neue` or 28cm Br N K (E).

Of these entire railway guns ever manufactured it was the 28cm Kanone 5 in Eisenbahnlafette or 28cm K 5 (E) that became the best railway gun ever built. The first gun entered service in 1936 and from then on it remained in production throughout the war with some 28 weapons having been made by 1945.

The manufacture of further railway guns continued with the production of a super heavy 38cm Kanone in Eisenbahnlafette `Siegfried` or 38cm Siegfried K (E). Four of these huge weapons were taken to Norway for coastal defence. These were also used for a short period as coast defence guns on the Hel Peninsula in Poland, protecting Danzig. However, by early 1942 they were withdrawn and redeployed as coast defence guns on turret mountings on the French coast.

A rare glimpse of a tracked 60cm Mörser gun named `Thor` being armed with 1.7-ton concrete piercing shells from a converted Pz.Kpfw.IV tank. Similar Morser`s were dispatched to the Eastern Front in July 1941 with the 628th schwere Artillerie Abteilung where it saw action at various sites, including Lemberg. The best-known action was against Sevastopol in 1942. Later, four guns were issued to the 833rd schwere Artillerie Abteilung. These guns had the names Adam, Eve (1st Battalion.) and Thor, Odin (2nd Battalion.) The names for guns V and VI were Loki and Ziu.

Another design of the super heavy railway gun that was also employed as a coast artillery weapon was the 40.6cm Kanone in Eisenbahnlafette `Adolf` or the 40.6cm Adolf K (E). This was an ex-naval gun, but production was delayed with only one ever being built.

The largest of the railway guns ever to be manufactured was the 80cm Kanone in Eisenbahnlafette `Gustav Gerat` or 80cm K (E). This monster gun weighing in at 1350-tons was capable of firing a 7-ton concrete-piercing shell some 23-miles.

In June 1942 `Gustav` was sent to the Eastern Front to Sevastopol where it fired 48 shots at various targets, all of which were totally destroyed. When the siege ended the gun was withdrawn and shipped back to Germany to have the barrel re-lined.

An identical 80cm K (E) gun code-named `Dora` was sent to southern Russia to Stalingrad in August 1942, but as fierce fighting grew it was soon withdrawn as the Red Army threatened the area with a counterattack.

A 21cm Mörser in its firing position during action on the Eastern Front in 1942. This powerful long range, counter-battery gun was mounted in a `mortar style` carriage that allowed very high elevation, as seen in this photograph.

A photograph taken at the moment the crew fires the Mörser. The gun is shrouded in dust and smoke after one of the projectiles is hurled from its long barrel miles into the enemy lines. Another shell is primed and ready for action and sits on a two-wheeled cradle.

A 21cm Mörser being prepared for firing. In spite of its size and long 38-ft barrel the gun is relatively well concealed between trees. This same carriage was used for the 17cm s. K 18 gun.

A Mörser fires one of its shells against any enemy target on the Eastern Front in 1942. This massive weapon has discharged a huge plume of smoke, which was undoubtedly detectable from the air. Of interest is how many crew manned this gun. Note the projectile on a two-wheeled cradle being moved over to the gun's special loading winching arm.

A railway gun in 1940. This monster gun was housed in a box-girder structure. Folding platforms and handrails were fitted and the assembly was mounted on two ten-wheel bogies. The Germans never used railway guns extensively during the war, but they were none-the-less a useful addition to coastal defences. The fact that they could also be moved by rail to a threatened sector was convenient, but the rail lines were constantly prone to aerial attack.

The crew of a 21cm Mörser protect their ears as the gun is fired. The huge blast reverberates their position as the projectile is hurled from the barrel. The 21cm Mörser was one of the largest calibre artillery pieces to be used by both the Wehrmacht and Waffen-SS.

A 21 Mörser during a lull in the fighting on the Eastern Front in 1942. Note the wicker artillery shipping containers stacked some distance from the gun. The Germans made extensive use of this low-cost material for ammunition containers.

A halftrack tows the barrel of a 21cm Mörser on its transporter during the summer of 1942. By this period of the war the production programme for the 21cm Mörser was cancelled as it was deemed no longer a viable weapon against the growing firepower of the Red Army.

A rare chance to see a monster Mörser being put through its paces during a training exercise in Germany in 1941. This super gun was never actually used in combat, but if the need ever arose it could have been dismantled on to ten railway flatcars. The operation to assemble the gun took about two hours.

The complete crew of a railway gun pose for the camera in 1943. These guns were primarily designed for long-range bombardment, but were too large to be permanently used on any war front, except for coastal defence.

A gun crew pose for the camera during operational duties on the Eastern Front in 1941. By the evidence of logs and a wooden platform especially constructed for the gun, the crew have utilised this position for containing the area through systematic heavy bombardments.

A log-framed shelter constructed to purposely house a heavy gun. Artillery shelters were common in Russia, especially on the Northern Front around Leningrad where the position would be used for some considerable time. The shelter was built to protect the gun, ammunition, and crew from the harsh winter.

A gunnery officer surveyors the terrain ahead after a 21cm Mörser devastates the surrounding countryside with a number of salvoes. The 21cm K 39 for instance was quite capable of firing a standard high explosive shell weighing some 135kgs to a maximum range of around 28,000-metres.

An artillery crew observe for themselves a crater caused by the impact of a 21cm high explosive shell. The size of the craters varied depending on the gun's range. A typical crater measured some 25-feet in circumference.

A gunner stands at the breech end of a heavy Mörser, which appears to be camouflaged by pieces of foliage. Larger guns like the 21cm and 24cm Mörser were not assigned to divisional artillery, but to army or corps level artillery formations, which could be tasked to support a division.

The crew of a 21cm Mörser are preparing the weapon to be transported after removing it from the carriage. For short distance movement the gun remained in one piece, but for longer moves it was normally split into two loads. For such moves the barrel was transported on a separate transport wagon.

A photograph taken of a heavy Mörser at the moment of firing during the winter of 1942 in Russia. Note the high elevation of the gun. These weapons were purposely designed to fire projectiles at higher than normal angles of elevation for long-range firing.

A Mörser in its elevated position prior to a firing mission on the Eastern Front in 1942. When not in action the gun was lowered over the piece to conceal it from aerial observation and protect the end of the barrel from dust particles and other foreign matter that could contaminate the weapon, reducing its firing capability.

A 21cm Mörser Waffen-SS gun crew relax in the heat of the Russian summer during operations in 1942. This was the largest calibre artillery piece to see action with the Waffen-SS. Only a few ever served in the select SS heavy artillery batteries at corps and army level.

Chapter Eight

Self-Propelled Gun Mounts

When Germany invaded Russia in 1941, its forces soon found itself hard pressed against Russian armour. The standard German towed light and medium anti-tank guns were proving ineffective against heavy Red Army tanks like the T-34 medium and KV-1 heavy tanks. As German forces advanced deeper across the uncharted wastelands of the Soviet Union, their forces became overstretched and increasingly vulnerable to Soviet armour. As a consequence the need for greater mobile anti-tank gun capability increased. In direct response to these needs came the self-propelled guns improvised as light tank hunters.

The origins of the self-propelled guns as light tank hunters came from German artillery demands for a highly mobile armoured infantry support vehicle that possessed a dual armour-piercing and high explosive capability. It was therefore decided that artillery pieces should be adapted and converted onto the chassis of armoured vehicles to produce a light tank hunter. By converting existing tank chassis' with self-propelled guns it enabled the artillery with a great deal of mobility, long range, good off-road capability and all-round fire that normal artillery guns could not achieve. All self-propelled guns that were to be mounted on the chassis of the tanks were to be in open hulls. Although they only offered limited protection against enemy fire, it reduced the weight of the self-propelled gun considerably, allowing it to travel further distances and climb steeper gradients than a normal tank. In order to sustain the self-propelled gun on the battlefield and keep up with the fast moving spearheads of a tank attack the vehicle was to be supported by tracked ammunition carriers.

One of the first vehicles to be fitted with an artillery piece was the 15cm schwere Infanteriegeschütz 33 or s. IG33 heavy infantry gun. This 15cm howitzer was mounted on the back of a Pz.Kpfw.I chassis, and was used not so much as a tank hunter, but as infantry support. It had a very effective gun, which could be fired at high or low elevations. Offensively, the s. IG33 were more than capable of accompanying attacking troops, and even provided direct fire against positions including armoured targets. However, by the time the s. IG33 saw action in Russia in 1941, the Germans quickly appreciated the need for a more powerful and potent self-propelled gun mounted vehicle.

At the end of 1941 the Germans had introduced the Marder or `Marten` series. These self-propelled vehicles were fitted with Germany`s most powerful anti-tank guns. The first of these weapons to be developed was the Sd.Kfz.139 Marder.III Panzerjäger (Tank Hunter). This vehicle mounted the captured Soviet 7.62cm M36 field gun and was married onto the chassis of the Pz.Kpfw.38 (t) Ausf.G tank. The Marder.III self-propelled gun had its first action in April 1942 and saw extensive fighting on the Eastern Front. Some 344 of these vehicles were manufactured and they quickly proved their worth against the Russian T-34 tank.

The success of the Marder.III led to the development during 1942 of a similar vehicle – the Sd.Kfz.138 Marder.III. This vehicle mounted the new German 7.5cm Pak 40/3 L/46 anti-tank gun on top of a Pz.Kpfw.38 (t) Ausf.H chassis. Later a modified version was introduced on an Ausf.M chassis.

The Marder. III series had proved a successful light tank hunter and the marriage of two powerful self-propelled guns fitted to the vehicle had given the Germans a mobile anti-tank capability that they so desperately needed.

Another tank chassis to be converted as a self-propelled anti-tank gun was the Pz.Kpfw.II tank. During the spring of 1942 the Pz.Kpfw.II. Ausf.D and Ausf.E variants mounted the 7.62cm M36 Soviet field gun, to produce the Panzerjäger.II Sd.Kfz.132 Marder.II. Later that year an additional 50 Ausf.F variants were converted. During this period further conversions were made with the introduction of the Sd.Kfz.131 Marder.II mounting the 7.62cm Pak 36r. Later conversions on the Pz.Kpfw.II chassis all carried the new powerful German 7.5cm Pak 40/2 anti-tank gun.

The success of the Marder.II and Marder.III series led to the development of a similar light tank hunter, the Marder.I. For this vehicle the Germans utilised the captured French Lorraine carrier chassis and converted a 7.5cm Pak 40 anti-tank gun over the vehicle's superstructure. Although the Marder.I principally served with German occupation forces in France, it still demonstrated its tank-killing prowess in the Normandy sector in June and July 1944.

Although the Marder series had quickly achieved notable success on the battlefield, there were other vehicles also of similar design that were equal or even better suited against heavy Russian armour. During 1941 and 1942 the production commenced with the `Wespe` or `Wasp`. The `Wespe` mounted the standard 10.5cm light field howitzer atop the standard Pz.Kpfw.II chassis. Between 1943 and late 1944 some 683 of these self-propelled tank hunters were built.

Another self-propelled tank hunter, which was the heaviest produced, was the `Hummel` or `Bumble Bee`. This vehicle mounted the standard 15cm heavy field howitzer atop the hybrid Pz.Kpfw.III and Pz.Kpfw.IV chassis. During its two-year production until 1944 some 666 `Hummel` self-propelled guns were constructed.

The 15cm heavy field howitzer was a very successful weapon and whilst the

Hummel was making its debut in Russia in 1942, so did another vehicle. This became known as the Sturminfanteriegeschütz 33 or the new s. IG33 infantry gun. The weapon was mounted on a rebuilt StuG.III chassis and saw service mainly in southern Russia between August 1942 and January 1943. Only 24 of these self-propelled gun-mounted weapons were ever produced and the majority were either destroyed or were captured during the battle of Stalingrad.

The success of the self-propelled gun mounted weapons saw further developments in their design. Once again the Germans found the dependable Czech Pz.Kpfw.38 (t) chassis as the platform for their new design, the Sd.Kfz.38 (t) Jagdpanzer `Hetzer`. This vehicle, which was built to replace the Marder, looked more like a steeply sloped, low-silhouetted tank than the normal standard open-topped tank hunter. It was fitted with a modified 7.5cm Pak 39 L/48 gun, and did not enter production until the spring of 1944. By the late summer of that year it began joining the Wehrmacht and Waffen-SS anti-tank battalions. The `Hetzer` performed well on the battlefield, but Germany's thirst to improve and increase the armoured punch saw the development of the heavy tank destroyers like the Jagdpanzer.V Jagdpanther and Jagdpanzer.IV. As for the self-propelled gun mounted vehicles like the S. IG33, Marder, Wespe, Hummel and Hetzer, they continued to serve in diminishing numbers until the end of the war.

A Hummel self-propelled tank destroyer is parked at a barracks in Poland in 1943. This vehicle has been mounted with the standard 15cm heavy field howitzer in a lightly armoured rear-fighting compartment atop the chassis of a Pz.Kpfw.IV tank.

The crew of a 7.62cm Pak36 (r) Marder.III self-propelled tank destroyer have halted in a field in Russia in 1943. This vehicle was a short term solution against superior Russian armour. A captured Russian 7.62cm gun was mounted on a Pz.Kpfw.38 (t). Eventually some 344 of these self-propelled vehicles were built. The Marder.III served mainly in Russia, although 66 were dispatched to North Africa.

A 7.62cm Pak36 (r) Marder.II advances along a road during the late winter of 1942. This captured anti-tank was mounted on a Pz.Kpfw.II tank. The vehicle's main protection for the four-man crew was provided by an extended gun shield.

Moving along a typical Russian road is a 7.62cm Pak36 (r) Marder.II. Unlike standard artillery, self-propelled guns were able to engage targets much quicker. These highly mobile tank destroyers were more mobile and proved more capable of supporting the armoured spearhead when called upon.

A 7.62cm Pak36 (r) Marder III travels across a field with its gun slightly elevated. Protective covering has been attached to protect the guns muzzle break indicating that the vehicle is not yet embroiled in combat.

On a training exercise is the Marder.II. The Marder II was a self-propelled anti-tank gun based on the obsolete Pz.Kpfw. II Ausf A/B/C and F light tank. This vehicle is armed with the 7.5cm PaK 40/2 L/46 anti-tank gun. It was designated 7.5cm PaK40/2 auf Fahrgestell Pz.Kpfw II (Sf).

A Nashorn self-propelled tank destroyer on the chassis of a Pz.Kpfw.IV tank advances through a town on the Eastern Front. The vehicle was developed as an interim solution in 1942, and was fitted with a potent 8.8cm 43/1 L/71 anti-tank gun. Though only lightly armoured and with a high profile, it stayed in service until the end of the war and proved to be a quite successful tank destroyer.

French civilians have mounted a well-camouflaged Jagdpanzer Hetzer 38 (t) self-propelled gun, which has obviously been abandoned by its crew after running out of fuel. The vehicle was armed with a 7.5cm Pak 39 L/46 gun and was better armored than the earlier Panzerjäger Marder and Nashorn with a thick steel sloped armoured front plate.

Two Jagdpanzer Hetzer 38 (t) self-propelled tank destroyers rumble through a town. The Hetzer 7.5cm Pak 39 gun was built on a specially widened Pz.Kpfw.38 (t) chassis. By the summer of 1944 this self-propelled gun began joining the both the Wehrmacht and Waffen-SS anti-tank battalions. In service the vehicle was mechanically reliable and small and easily concealed. However, its main failings were the cramped working conditions for the crew.

A long column of Nashorn self-propelled guns secured on railway flatcars is destined for the front lines in Russia in 1943. The development of the famous 8.8cm anti-aircraft gun, which was mounted on the rear of the chassis complete with its gun shield and an open topped superstructure, became a very successful anti-tank weapon on the battlefield.

A 7.62cm Pak36 (r) Marder.II self-propelled anti-tank gun has halted in a field near a StuG.III. Ausf.G. This particular Marder is based on the Pz.Kpfw. II light tank, but on the Ausf D/E and Flammpanzer II variants. This improvised tank hunter was developed in response for the need for more mobile anti-tank firepower.

Hummel self-propelled tank destroyers have been secured and ready for their journey East during early 1944. The Hummel weighed some 23-tons, and to limit weight the vehicle carried just 18 15cm rounds. From the spring of 1943 a single battery of six Hummel plus a Hummel munitions carrier were allocated to Wehrmacht and Waffen-SS Panzer divisions.

Three armed crewmen pose for the camera in front of their Marder.II. By the end of 1942 the success of mounting standard artillery pieces to the chassis of a tank prompted the Germans to increase the demand for more of these mobile artillery tank destroyers.

A schwere Infanteriegeschütz 33 or s. IG33 armoured vehicle can be seen parked to the right of a Pz.Kpfw.I during the French campaign in 1940. The s. IG33 was an infantry support weapon, and possessed the bulk of a 15cm howitzer. Through the war, especially during the early periods these pieces provided valuable firepower for both offensive and defensive actions.

A Hummel being prepared to be shipped out East. This self-propelled vehicle proved an effective improvisation that married the powerful 15cm howitzer with a readily available platform to provide German troops with mobile anti-tank capability they so desperately required.

A Marder in action as it fires its lethal 7.62cm anti-tank gun against a Soviet target in 1943. The Marder II served extensively in both Wehrmacht and Waffen-SS divisional anti-tank battalions, particularly on the Eastern Front. In the battalions it served it quickly proved its tactical worth.

The crew of a Sturminfanteriegeschütz 33 pose for the camera during a pause in their advance. This rare vehicle mounted the 15cm s. IG33 infantry gun on a re-built StuG.III chassis. A total of 24 were built and although they were primarily to support infantry, they were also used to neutralise enemy armour. However, many were lost with the surrender of the German 6.Armee at Stalingrad in early 1943.